New York
Total Eclipse Guide

Official Commemorative 2024 Keepsake Guidebook

2024 Total Eclipse State Guide Series

Aaron Linsdau

Sastrugi Press

Jackson Hole

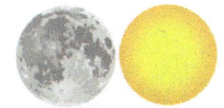

Copyright © 2018 by Aaron Linsdau

All rights reserved. No part of this book may be reproduced or transmitted in any form or by any means, electronic or mechanical, including photocopying, recording, or by any computer system without the written permission of the author, except where permitted by law.

Sastrugi Press / Published by arrangement with the author

New York Total Eclipse Guide: Official Commemorative 2024 Keepsake Guidebook

    The author has made every effort to accurately describe the locations contained in this work. Travel to some locations in this book is hazardous. The publisher has no control over and does not assume any responsibility for author or third-party websites or their content describing these locations, how to travel there, nor how to do it safely. Refer to local regulations and laws.

    Any person exploring these locations is personally responsible for checking local conditions prior to departure. You are responsible for your own actions and decisions. The information contained in this work is based solely on the author's research at the time of publication and may not be accurate in the future. Neither the publisher nor the author assumes any liability for anyone climbing, exploring, visiting, or traveling to the locations described in this work. Climbing is dangerous by its nature. Any person engaging in mountain climbing is responsible for learning the proper techniques. The reader assumes all risks and accepts full responsibility for injuries, including death.

Sastrugi Press
PO Box 1297, Jackson, WY 83001, United States
www.sastrugipress.com
Quantity sales: Special discounts are available on quantity purchases by corporations, associations, and others. For details, contact the publisher at the address above.

Library of Congress Catalog-in-Publication Data
Library of Congress Control Number: 2018905467
Linsdau, Aaron
New York Total Eclipse Guide / Aaron Linsdau-1st United States edition
p. cm.
1. Nature 2. Astronomy 3. Travel 4. Photography
Summary: Learn everything you need to know about viewing, experiencing, and photographing the total eclipse in New York on April 8, 2024.

ISBN-13: 978-1-64922-319-7 (paperback)

508.4—dc23

All photography, maps and artwork by the author, except as noted.

10 9 8 7 6

Contents

Introduction	4
All About New York	6
Overview of New York	6
Weather	11
Finding the Right Location	13
Road Closures and Traffic	14
Wilderness and Forest Park Safety	15
Eclipse Day Safety	17
All About Eclipses	19
Total vs Partial Eclipse	20
Early Myth & Astronomy	22
Contemporary American Solar Phenomena	24
Future American Eclipses	26
Viewing and Photographing the Eclipse	27
Planning Ahead	28
Understanding Sun Position	29
Eclipse Data for Selected Locations	31
Eclipse Photography	31
Eclipse Photography Gear	34
Camera Phones	36
Viewing Locations Around New York	43
Remember the New York Total Eclipse	65

Introduction

Thank you for purchasing this book. It has everything you need to know about the total eclipse in New York on April 8, 2024.

A total eclipse passing through the United States is a rare event. The last US total eclipse was in 2017. It traveled from Oregon to South Carolina. The last American total eclipse prior to that was in 1979!

The next total eclipse over the US will not be until April 8, 2024. It will pass over Texas, the Midwest, and on to Maine. After that, the next coast-to-coast total eclipse will be in 2045.

It's imperative to make travel plans early. You will be amazed at the number of people swarming to the total eclipse path. Some might say watching a partial versus a total eclipse is a similar experience. It's not.

This book is written for New York visitors and anyone else viewing the eclipse. You will find general planning, viewing, and photography information inside. Should you travel to the eclipse path in New York in April, be prepared for an epic trip. The estimates based on the 2017 eclipse suggest that millions will converge on Upstate New York.

Some hotels in the communities and cities along the path of totality in New York have already been contacted by people to make reservations. Finding lodging along the eclipse path may be a major challenge.

Resources will be stretched far beyond the normal limits. Think gas lines from the late 1970s. It may be likely that traffic along highways will come to a complete standstill during this event. Be prepared with backup supplies.

Many smaller New York towns are far from any major city. New York country roads can be slow. Please obey posted speed limits for the safety of everyone. Be cautious about believing a map application's estimate of travel time in New York.

People in communities along the path of the total eclipse may rent out properties for this event. With this major celestial spectacle in the spring of 2024, be assured that New York "hasn't seen anything yet."

Is this to say to avoid New York or other areas during the eclipse? Not at all! This guidebook provides ideas for interesting, alternative, and memorable locations to see the eclipse. It will be too late to rush to a better spot once the eclipse begins. Law enforcement will be out to help drivers reconsider speeding.

Please be patient and careful. There will be a large rush of people from all over the world, converging on New York to enjoy the total eclipse. Be mindful of other drivers on eclipse weekend, as they may not be familiar with New York roads.

You should feel compelled to play hooky on April 8. Ask for the day off. Take your kids out of school. They'll be adults before the next chance to see a total eclipse over America. Create family memories that will last a lifetime. Sastrugi Press does not normally advocate skipping school or work. Make an exception because this is too big an event to miss.

Wherever you plan to be along the total eclipse path, leave early and remember your eclipse glasses. People from all around the planet will converge on New York. Be good to your fellow humans and be safe. We all want to enjoy this spectacular show.

Visit www.sastrugipress.com/eclipse for the latest updates for the state eclipse book series.

Author Information

Polar explorer and motivational speaker Aaron Linsdau's first book, *Antarctic Tears*, is an emotional journey into the heart of Antarctica. He ate two sticks of butter every day to survive. Aaron coughed up blood early in the expedition and struggled with equipment failures. Despite the endless difficulties, he set a world record for surviving the longest solo expedition to the South Pole.

Aaron teaches how to build resilience to overcome adversity by managing attitude. He shares his techniques for overcoming adrenaline burnout and constant overload. He inspires audiences to face their challenges with a new perspective. As a motivational speaker, Aaron talks about courage, resilience, attitude, safety, and risk. He hopes that you will be inspired and have an enjoyable time watching the total eclipse in New York.

Visit his websites at www.aaronlinsdau.com or www.ncexped.com.

All About New York

OVERVIEW OF NEW YORK

The state of New York is one of the original thirteen colonies of the United States and continues to dominate the cultural and financial scene of the country. The city of New York is the most populated city in the USA. It is home to some of the world's spectacular architectural designs. Upstate New York is home to the most beautiful farms and vineyards, rugged trails, clear lakes, and magnificent waterfalls. Upstate New York is made up of vast agricultural lands. The area produces lots of milk, apples, and wine from its vineyards. As of 2018, New York State's total population was approximately nineteen million while only eight million people live in Upstate New York.

When planning to visit the area in the spring, it is good to remember that Upstate may still be chilly compared to the rest of the state. Brace yourself with warm clothing to ward off the chill, depending on the springtime conditions. During summer, you can enjoy your vacation by hiking the mountains and enjoying beautiful terrain. Some favorite trails include the Devil's Path in the Catskills and the Whiteface Mountain Steps, a set of human-made steps in the Adirondack Mountains. As you climb, you get a chance to take great pictures to capture your memories. The Devil's Path will surely make you sweat, but you will get a spectacular view from Twin Mountain, Plateau Mountain, or the Indian Head.

Although some of the names mentioned here might not be familiar, the areas have beautiful sites that even Hollywood producers have used when filming their movies. Buffalo is one such area of Upstate New York that is home to the most spectacular waterfalls. While at

Buffalo, ensure that you spare time to visit Niagara Falls, one of the world's greatest wonders. The falls are located on the border of the United States and Canada. You can choose to view the fantastic waterfall from above on a helicopter, by boat, or even behind the falls in a tunnel. Either way, the view is remarkable.

The Adirondacks are a perfect place for those looking for an escape during the fall. The area is full of hills with hundreds of peaks, allowing you the opportunity to watch the trees change colors. You can enjoy canoeing sports at the many lakes in the hills or rent a fishing boat and have fun with your family and friends. For a place to stay while here, you can choose a condo that is near a lake or just bring along your camping gear.

A walk along the beaches of Lake Erie during the evening hours is one of the most beautiful things you can do. The stunning sunsets over sandy beaches give the lake a sense of tranquility. If you want to enjoy the lake from an elevated place, many photogenic lighthouses surround Lake Erie.

As for drinks, Upstate New York has several vineyards. At the heart of Dundee next to Finger Lakes is McGregor Vineyard. Stand in the middle of the yard and breathe in the fresh breeze from the lake combined with the sweet smell of the ripe grapes. You will fall in love with upcountry life. Another great vineyard is in Rochester on the Niagara Wine Trail. It is close to many restaurants and a B&B for a night's stay. The Wine Trail has produced many fine wines and won several awards. Come prepared to taste and carry some home.

For more aquatic moments, find your way to St. Lawrence River. The river stretches from Ontario, Canada to the Adirondacks. The river has multiple islands along its length. The area has the most beautiful holiday condos and magnificent summer homes. A ride along the river highlights a view of the unique islands. Many islands on the river are privately owned, but a substantial number are open to the public. Plan to visit the area during summer months. As if that is not enough, Skaneateles hosts a 120-acre lavender farm. You will be awed by the architectural mastery of Graycliff Estate located in Derby. The Buffalo area and all along the Great Lakes are famous for deep snowfalls during the winter. By April, the snow should be nearly gone, so you should only need to prepare for cool temperatures and potentially rainy conditions during the eclipse.

The beauty of Upstate New York is not only defined by natural features but human made as well. The people are welcoming and warm and ready to guide you when you visit. Be prepared for a unique American experience during the 2024 total eclipse.

Hotels and Motels During the Eclipse

Once excitement of the total eclipse over New York spreads, rooms will become scarce. Many hotels in towns along the path of totality in western states sold out a year in advance for the 2017 total eclipse. New York is not alone in this challenge. Hotels all along the path of totality will sell out in anticipation of the 2024 total eclipse.

What does this mean for eclipse visitors? Lodging and room rentals in eclipse towns will be at a massive premium. Does that mean all hope is lost to find a place to stay? Not at all. But you will have to be creative. There will be few, if any, hotel rooms available in these eclipse cities by early 2024. Accommodations in the cities and towns along the path of the eclipse will be difficult to come by.

In summer 2017, the author searched on Hotels.com for rooms along the 2017 total eclipse path on the weekend of August 21 and found many major cities sold out. Once word of the 2024 eclipse spreads, room rates will increase and availability will drop.

Search for rooms farther away from the eclipse path. If you are willing to stay in cities outside the eclipse path, you will have better success at finding rooms. As the eclipse approaches, people will book rooms farther from the totality path. By early spring, rooms in cities near the total eclipse path may be unavailable. The effect of this event will be felt across New York and the rest of the United States.

Think regionally when looking for rooms. Be prepared to search far and wide during this major event. If a five-hour drive is manageable, your lodging options greatly expand, but it also increases your travel risk.

Internet Rentals

To find rooms to stay in towns along the eclipse path, try a web service such as Airbnb.com. Note that some people rent out rooms or homes illegally, against zoning regulations. Cities will feel the crunch of inquiries early due to others who experienced the 2017 eclipse.

If cities fully enforce zoning laws, authorities may prevent your weekend home rental. Online home rentals during the eclipse will be a target for rental scams. People from out of the area steal photos and descriptions, then post the home for rent. You send your check or wire money to a "rental agent" then show up to find you have been scammed. If the deal sounds strange or too good to be true, run away.

Camping

If you can book a campsite, do it as soon as you can. Do not wait. All areas in the national forests are first-come, first-served. Forest roads may be packed. Expect all areas to be swarming with people. Show up early to stake out your spot. Consider staying farther away and driving early on April 8.

Please respect private land too. New York folks don't take kindly to people overrunning their property without permission. In a big state with millions of residents, people are very protective, but they're friendly, too. You never know what you might be able to arrange with a smile and a bit of money.

This all said, there are plenty of camping opportunities throughout New York. You don't have to sleep exactly on the eclipse path. If you're ready to rough it, there are national forest camping options.

Government agencies will meet years in advance to talk about how to manage the influx of people. Every possible government agency will be working full time to enforce the various rules and regulations.

National Parks and Monuments

Finding a camping site at any state park, national park, or national monument along the eclipse path in New York will be challenging. To watch the eclipse from any location, you do not have to sleep in it. You just need to drive there in the morning.

Law enforcement will be present on the eclipse weekend. Hundreds of thousands of people are expected in the region. Parking may overflow. It will make parking lots and lines on Black Friday at the mall look uncrowded. For an event of this magnitude, find your location as early as possible.

The first sentence of the national parks mission statement is:
"The National Park Service preserves unimpaired the natural and cultural resources and values of the national park system for the enjoyment, education, and inspiration of this and future generations."

Roadside camping (sleeping in your car) is not allowed in national monuments or parks. Park facilities are only designed to handle so many people per day. Water, trash collection, and toilets can only withstand so much. If you notice trash on the ground, take a moment to throw it away. Protect your national park and help out. Rangers are diligent and hardworking but they can only do so much to manage the expected crowds.

National Forests and Wilderness

There are national forest options in New York. They all have camping opportunities. The forest service manages undeveloped and primitive campsites. Be sure to check for any fire restrictions. Check with individual agencies for last-minute information and regulations. The forest service requires proper food storage. Plan to purchase food and water before choosing your campsite. Below is the information for the national forest in New York State.

Finger Lakes National Forest

https://www.fs.usda.gov/main/gmfl/home
https://www.dec.ny.gov/outdoor/66666.html

Backcountry service roads abound in New York. Maps for forests are available at local visitor centers and bookstores. This book's website has digital copies of some forest maps.

Printed national forest maps are large and detailed. They have illustrated road paths, connections, and other vital travel information not available on digital device maps. Viewing digital maps on your smartphone or mobile pad is difficult. If you plan to camp in the forest, a real paper map is a wise investment.

Camping in federal wilderness areas is also allowed. Those areas afford the ultimate backcountry experience. However, be aware that no vehicle travel is allowed in the specially designated areas. This ban includes: vehicles, bikes, hang gliders, and drones. You can travel only on foot or with pack animals.

Sleep in Your Car

Countless RVs, campers, trucks, cars, and motorcycles will flood New York. Sleeping in your car with friends is tolerable. Doing so with unadventurous spouses or children is another matter.

Do not be caught along the path of the total eclipse without some sort of plan, especially in the bigger cities of New York. The whole path of totality will fill with people on April 8.

Useful Local Webcams

Local webcams are handy to make last-minute travel decisions. Modern webcams are sensitive enough to show headlights at night. Use them to determine if there are issues before traveling out. Eclipse traffic will add to the morning commuter traffic.

There are smartphone applications which are useful to check webcams in many locations. Consult your device's app store for the latest updates. Whether you use an app or computer, an Internet search will reveal many handy webcams for your eclipse planning.

Weather

It's all about the weather during the eclipse. Nothing else will matter if the sky is cloudy. You can be nearly anywhere along the path in New York and catch a view of the event when traffic comes to a standstill. But if there's a cloud cover forecast, seriously reconsider your viewing location.

Travel early wherever you plan to go. Attempting to change locations an hour before the eclipse due to weather will likely cause you to miss the event. New York country roads can be narrow and slow. The number of vehicles will cause unexpected backups.

Modern Forecasts

Use a smartphone application to check the up-to-date weather. Wunderground is a good application and has relatively reliable forecasts for the region. The hourly forecast for the same day has been rather accurate for the last two years. The below discussion refers to features found in the Wunderground app. However, any application with detailed weather views will improve your eclipse forecasting skills.

Cloud Cover Forecast

The most useful forecast view is the visible and infrared cloud-coverage map. Avoid downloading this app the night before and trying to learn how to read it. Practice reading them at home. It's imperative to understand how to interpret the maps early.

Infrared cloud map showing the worst case eclipse cloud cover. Courtesy of National Weather Service.

All cloud cover, night or day, will appear on an infrared map. Warm, low-altitude clouds are shown in white and gray. High-altitude cold clouds are displayed in shades of green, yellow, red, and purple. Anything other than a clear map spells eclipse-viewing problems.

To improve your weather guess, use the animated viewer of the cloud cover. It will give you a sense of cloud motion. You can discern whether clouds or rain are moving toward, away from, or circulating around your location.

Normal New York Weather Pattern

Due to the direction of the jet stream, most weather travels across the Pacific Ocean, through the western states, over the Midwest, and then into New York. On occasion, weather can approach from Canada or from the Atlantic. Due to the nature of the tropical storms from the Atlantic, weather in New York can be unpredictable.

The common weather pattern in April is slightly warm in the afternoon and mildly cool in the evenings. Passing cold fronts in spring can bring unexpected cloud cover and rains.

Historically, New York tends to have moderate cloud cover during April. Prepare to make adjustments. If anything other than clear skies are predicted, drive to other parts of New York, Ohio, or Vermont.

Be aware of severe weather in New York. Although winter is generally over by April, there have been nor'easter storms in this month. Pay attention to the weather forecast. If dangerous weather is predicted, your main concern should be safety rather than chasing an eclipse.

Consider that slow-moving clouds can obscure the sun for far longer than the four-minute duration of the totality. The time of totality is so short that you do not want to risk it. Missing it due to a single cloud will be a major disappointment.

Local Eclipse Weather Forecasts

Local town and city newspapers, radio, and television stations around New York will have a weekend edition with articles discussing the eclipse weather. However, conditions change unpredictably in New York. A three-day forecast for April may be incorrect.

Finding the Right Location to View Eclipse Effects

One of the peculiarities of total eclipses is that the entire show is not only in the sky. There are other unusual effects seen during the total eclipse that are worth looking for.

The first effect to watch for is the crescent moon shapes created from leaf shadows on the ground. They're best viewed on a sidewalk or asphalt. They can only be observed during the partial eclipse. The other effect that is worth watching for is the shadow bands or "snakes" as they're commonly called.

Shadow banding is seen right before and after the totality takes place. They're best observed on smooth, plain-colored surfaces. If you plan to be in the forest for the eclipse, you may struggle to see the bands but will likely see crescent shadows all around on the ground.

One of the supreme challenges with all of these effects is choosing what to watch. You can see the crescent shadows in the hour before and after the totality but shadow banding happens before or after totality. It is more difficult to look away from the eclipse than you think.

Road Closures and Traffic

Highways connecting various New York towns in the total eclipse path will be heavily impacted on the weekend before and day of the eclipse. As was found in the 2017 total eclipse, there is no way to predict which areas will be impacted.

Planning ahead is essential to give you the best opportunity to enjoy the eclipse without the nightmare of being stuck in traffic for hours on end. The traffic in Oregon and Idaho was stunning, so imagine what it will be like for New York.

Update yourself with the latest road report information from the New York road condition website:

https://511ny.org

It's imperative to plan early and have one if not more backup plans in case of difficult travel conditions. April weather is unpredictable and variable.

If you believe it's necessary to leave a town to watch the eclipse, do so the night before or extremely early in the morning. RVs are common, and trains of them crawl through popular areas.

New York Information

Cellular Phones

Cellular "cell" phone service in remote New York locations may be problematic. Most of the time there is good coverage along the main highways and interstates. However, even along major thoroughfares, there can be little or no coverage.

It's possible to find zones where text messages will send when phone calls are impossible. If you cannot make a phone call, the chance of having data coverage for web surfing or e-mail is low.

Please look up any information or communicate what you need before departing from the main roads around New York. Bureau of Land Management (BLM) areas sometimes have coverage. Planned to be self-contained. Plan for your cell phone not to connect.

You may find yourself out of cell service. With a large number of cell users in a concentrated area, coverage and data speed may collapse as well. Search on the phrase "cell phone coverage breathing".

Wilderness and Forest Safety

All New York mountains and wilderness areas are full of wild animals. Although beautiful, wild animals can be dangerous. They can easily injure or kill people, as they are far more powerful than humans. Do not try to feed any wild animals, including squirrels, foxes, and chipmunks, as they can carry diseases. These suggestions apply to all public lands.

Feral Hogs

Introduced in the early twentieth century, hogs have become a potential problem in New York. Although they tend to flee when encountered, hogs have been known to attack people. They can be aggressive and their tusks can inflict serious wounds. There have been instances of deaths, too. It is best to leave these animals alone if you encounter one.

Moose

This member of the deer family is extremely defensive when they are with their young. If you see a calf moose, leave the area as soon as you can. If a moose approaches, back away. Put something between you and the moose. Unlike bears, it is okay to run from moose. Stay at least twenty-five yards away from moose.

Venomous Snakes

There are multiple species of venomous snakes in New York including the Timber Rattlesnake, Massasauga rattlesnake, and the

Copperhead. Although these reptiles are not generally aggressive, they can strike when provoked or threatened. Of the approximately 8,000 people annually bitten by venomous snakes in the United States, ten to fifteen people die according to the U.S. Food and Drug Administration.

The best way to avoid rattlesnake encounters is to be mindful of your environment. Do not place your hands or feet in locations where you cannot clearly see the surroundings. Avoid heavy brush or tall weeds where snakes hide during the day. Step on a log or rock rather than over it, as a hidden snake might be on the other side. Rattlesnakes may not make any noise before striking.

Avoid handling all snakes. Should you be bitten, stay calm and call 911 or emergency dispatch as soon as possible. Transport the victim to the nearest medical facility immediately. Rapid professional treatment is the best way to manage rattlesnake bites. Refer to U.S. Forest Service and professional medical texts for more information on managing rattlesnakes injuries.

Bears

The forests of New York are home to black bears. Safety is imperative around these powerful animals. Although they often appear docile, they can become aggressive if threatened. In the unlikely event of an attack, fight back against the bear. Use whatever you have at your disposal to defend yourself. Report all negative or aggressive bears to the local authorities.

If a bear hears you, it will usually vacate the area. Bear charges are often caused by unexpected and surprise encounters. Noise is the best defense to avoid surprising bears. Regularly clap, make noise, and talk loudly. The New York Department of Environmental Conservation website has more specific information on safety and food management in bear country at https://www.dec.ny.gov/animals/6960.html.

It is recommended to stay one hundred yards (300 feet) away from all bears. They are exciting to see but need their space. Refer to current forest or park regulations for more safety information.

Ticks

Ticks exist all across the United States but not all species transmit disease. Ticks cannot fly or jump, but they climb grasses in shrubs in order to attach to people or animals that pass by. Ticks feed on the blood of their host. In doing so, they can transmit potentially life-threatening diseases such as Lyme disease.

Eclipse Day Safety

1. Hydrate

Spring temperatures are usually mild to warm. The excitement of the event can distract you from managing hydration. Drink plenty of water. Consume more than you would at home.

2. Eye Safety time

Use certified eclipse safety glasses at all times when viewing the partial eclipse. Only remove the glasses when the totality happens. Give your eyes time to rest. They can dry out and become irritated. Bring FDA approved eye drops to keep your eyes moist.

3. Sun exposure

Facing at the sun for three hours can result in sunburns. Wear sunglasses and liberally apply sunscreen to avoid sunburns.

4. Eat well

Keep your energy up. Appetite loss is common when traveling. Maintain your normal eating schedule.

5. Prepare for temperature changes

Temperatures will drop rapidly during the eclipse and also once the sun sets. Bring appropriate clothing.

6. Talk with your doctor

If the sun exposure, insects, or heat bothers you talk with your doctor before traveling. Seek professional medical attention for serious symptoms.

Total eclipse path across the United States (approximate).

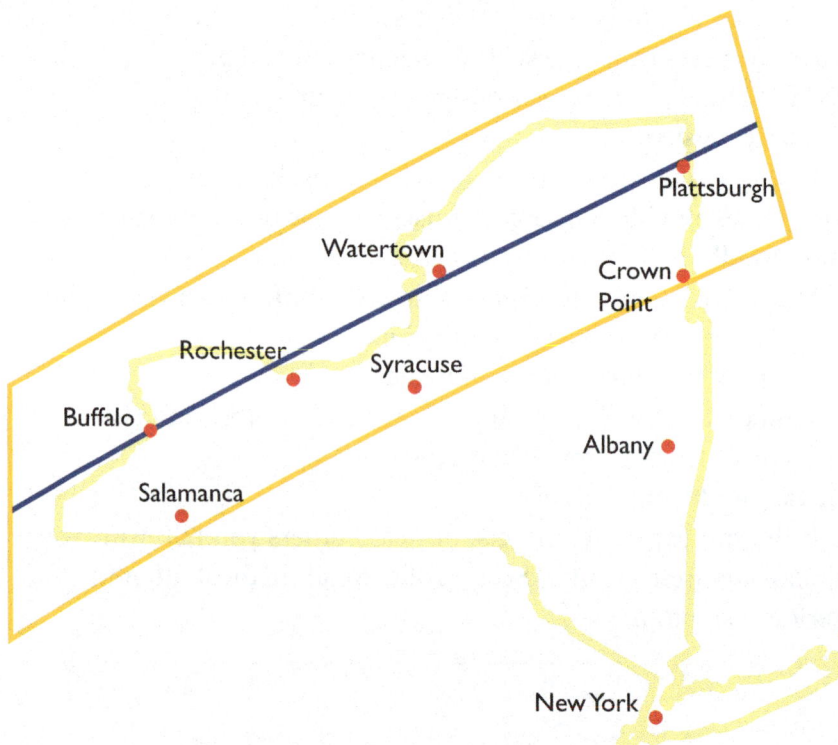

Total eclipse path across New York (approximate).

All About Eclipses

How an Eclipse Happens

An eclipse occurs when one celestial body falls in line with another, thus obscuring the sun from view. This occurs much more often than you'd think, considering how many bodies there are in the solar system. For instance, there are over 150 moons in the solar system. On Earth, we have two primary celestial bodies: the sun and the moon. The entire solar system is constantly in motion, with planets orbiting the sun and moons orbiting the planets. These celestial bodies often come into alignment. When these alignments cause the sun to be blocked, it is called an eclipse.

For an eclipse to occur, the sun, Earth, and moon must be in alignment. There are two types of eclipses: solar and lunar. A solar eclipse occurs when the moon obscures the sun. A lunar eclipse occurs when the moon passes through Earth's shadow. Solar eclipses are much more common, as we experience an average of 240 solar eclipses a century compared to an average of 150 lunar eclipses. Despite this, we are more likely to see a lunar eclipse than a solar eclipse. This is due to the visibility of each.

For a solar eclipse to be visible, you have to be in the moon's shadow. The problem with viewing a total eclipse is that the moon casts a small shadow over the world at any given time. You have to be in

* ILLUSTRATION NOT TO SCALE

a precise location to view a total eclipse. The issue that arises is that most of these locations are inaccessible to most people. Though many would like to see a total solar eclipse, most aren't about to set sail for the middle of the Pacific Ocean. In fact, a solar eclipse is visible in the same place on the world on average every 375 years. This means that if you miss a solar eclipse above your hometown, you're not going to see another one unless you travel or move.

It's much easier to catch a glimpse of a lunar eclipse, even though they occur at a much lower frequency than their solar counterparts. A lunar eclipse darkens the moon for a few hours. This is different than a new moon when it faces away from the sun. During these eclipses, the moon fades and becomes nearly invisible.

Another result of a lunar eclipse is a blood moon. Earth's atmosphere bends a small amount of sunlight onto the moon turning it orange-red. The blood moon is caused by the dawn or dusk light being refracted onto the moon during an eclipse.

Lunar eclipses are much easier to see. Even when the moon is in the shadow of Earth, it's still visible throughout the world because of how much smaller it is than Earth.

Total vs. Partial Eclipse

What is the difference between a partial and total eclipse? A total eclipse of either the sun or the moon will occur only when the sun, Earth, and the moon are aligned in a perfectly straight line. This ensures that either the sun or the moon is partially or completely obscured.

In contrast, a partial eclipse occurs when the alignment of the three celestial bodies is not in a perfectly straight line. These types of eclipses usually result in only a part of either the sun or the moon being obscured. This is often what led to ancient civilizations believing that some form of magical beast or deity was eating the sun or the moon. It appears as though something has taken a bite out of either the sun or the moon during a partial eclipse.

Total eclipses, rarer than partial eclipses, still occur quite often. It's more difficult for people to be in a position to experience such an event firsthand. Total solar eclipses can only be viewed from a small portion of the world that falls into the darkest part of the moon's shadow. Often this happens in the middle of the ocean.

The Moon's Shadow

The moon's shadow is divided into two parts: the umbra and the penumbra. The former is much smaller than the latter, as the umbra is the innermost and darkest part of the shadow. The umbra is thus the central point of the moon's shadow, meaning that it is extremely small in comparison to the entire shadow. For a total solar eclipse to be visible, you need to be directly beneath the umbra of the moon's shadow. This is because that is the only point at which the moon completely blocks the view of the sun.

In contrast, the penumbra is the region of the moon's shadow in which only a portion of the light cast by the sun is obscured. When

Total eclipse shadow 2016 as seen from 1 million miles on the Deep Space Climate Observatory satellite. Courtesy of NASA.

standing in the penumbra, you are viewing the eclipse at an angle. In the penumbra, the moon does not completely block the sun from view. This means that while the event is a total solar eclipse, you'll only see a partial eclipse. The umbra for the April 8 eclipse is over one hundred miles wide. The penumbra will cover much of the United States.

To provide some context, one total solar eclipse we experienced occurred on March 9, 2016, and was visible as a partial eclipse across most of the Pacific Ocean, parts of Asia, and Australia. However, the only place in the world to view this total solar eclipse was in a few parts of Indonesia.

Due to the varied locations and the brief periods for which they're visible, it's difficult to see each and every eclipse that occurs. The umbra of the moon is such a small fraction of the entire shadow and the majority of our planet is comprised of water. Thus, the rarity of being able to view a total solar eclipse increases significantly because it's likely that the umbra will fall over some part of the ocean rather than a populated landmass. There are not total or annular eclipses every month because the moon's orbit is 5.1° off the ecliptic plane of the Earth and sun.

Eclipses Throughout History

Ancient peoples believed eclipses were from the wrath of angry gods, portents of doom and misfortune, or wars between celestial beings. Eclipses have played many roles in cultures, creating myths since the dawn of time. Both solar and lunar eclipses affected societies worldwide. Inspiring fear, curiosity, and the creation of legends, eclipses have cast a long shadow in the collective unconscious of humanity throughout history.

Early Myth & Astronomy

Documented observations of solar eclipses have been found as far back in history as ancient Egyptian and Chinese records. Timekeeping was important to ancient Chinese cultures. Astronomical observations were an integral factor in the Chinese calendar. The first observation of a solar eclipse is found in Chinese records from over 4,000 years ago. Evidence suggests that ancient Egyptian observations may predate those archaic writings.

Many ancient societies, including Roman, Greek and Chinese civilizations, were able to infer and foresee solar eclipses from astronomical data. The sudden and unpredictable nature of solar eclipses had a stressful and intimidating effect on many societies that lacked the scientific insight to accurately predict astronomical events. Relying on the sun for their agricultural livelihood, those societies interpreted solar eclipses as world-threatening disasters.

In ancient Vietnam, solar eclipses were explained as a giant frog eating the sun. The peasantry of ancient Greece believed that an eclipse was the sign of a furious godhead, presenting an omen of wrathful retribution in the form of natural disasters. Other cultures were less speculative in their investigations. The Chinese Song Dynasty scientist Shen Kuo proved the spherical nature of the Earth and heavenly bodies through scientific insight gained by the study of eclipses.

The Eclipse in Native American Mythology

Eclipses have played a significant role in the history of the United States. Before Europeans settled in the Americas, solar eclipses were important astronomical events to Native American cultures. In most native cultures, an eclipse was a particularly bad omen. Both the sun and the moon were regarded as sacred. Viewing an eclipse, or even being outside for the duration of the event, was considered highly taboo by the Navajo culture. During an eclipse, men and women would simply avert their eyes from the sky, acting as though it was not happening.

The Choctaw people had a unique story to explain solar eclipses. Considering the event as the mischievous actions of a black squirrel and its attempt to eat the sun, the Choctaw people would do their best to scare away the cosmic squirrel by making as much noise as

possible until the end of the event, at which point cognitive bias would cause them to believe they'd once again averted disaster on an interplanetary scale.

Contemporary American Solar Phenomena

The investigation of solar phenomena in twentieth-century American history had a similarly profound effect on the people of the United States. A total solar eclipse occurring on the sixteenth of June, 1806, engulfed the entire country. It started near modern-day Arizona. It passed across the Midwest, over Ohio, Pennsylvania, New York, Massachusetts, and Connecticut. The 1806 total eclipse was notable for being one of the first publicly advertised solar events. The public was informed beforehand of the astronomical curiosity through a pamphlet written by Andrew Newell entitled *Darkness at Noon, or the Great Solar Eclipse*.

This pamphlet described local circumstances and went into great detail explaining the true nature of the phenomenon, dispelling myth and superstition, and even giving questionable advice on the best methods of viewing the sun during the event. Replete with a short historical record of eclipses through the ages, the *Darkness at Noon* pamphlet is one of the first examples of an attempt to capitalize on the mysterious nature of solar eclipses.

Another notable American solar eclipse occurred on June 8, 1918. Passing over the United States from Washington to Florida, the eclipse was accurately predicted by the U.S. Naval Observatory and heavily documented in the newspapers of the day. Howard Russell Butler, painter and founder of the American Fine Arts Society, painted the eclipse from the U.S. Naval Observatory, immortalizing the event in *The Oregon Eclipse*.

Four more total solar eclipses occurred over the United States in the years 1923, 1925, 1932, and 1954, with another occurring in 1959. The October 2, 1959, solar eclipse began over Boston, Massachusetts. It was a sunrise event that was unviewable from the ground level. Eminent astronomer Jay Pasachoff attributed this event to sparking his interest in the study of astronomy. Studying under Professor Donald Menzel of Williams College, Pasachoff was able to view the event from an airline hired by his professor.

To this day, many myths surround the eclipse. In India, some local customs require fasting. In eastern Africa, eclipses are seen as a danger to pregnant women and young children. Despite the mystery and legend associated with unique and rare astronomical events, eclipses continue to be awe-inspiring. Even in the modern day, eclipses draw out reverential respect for the inexorable passing of celestial bodies. They are a reminder of the intimate relationship between the denizens of Earth and the universe at large.

Present Day Eclipses

The year 2017 brought the world's most-watched total eclipse in history on August 21, when a total solar eclipse crossed the United States. An annular eclipse, a "ring of fire," will pass over the United States in 2023 from Oregon to Texas. Though impressive, it will not

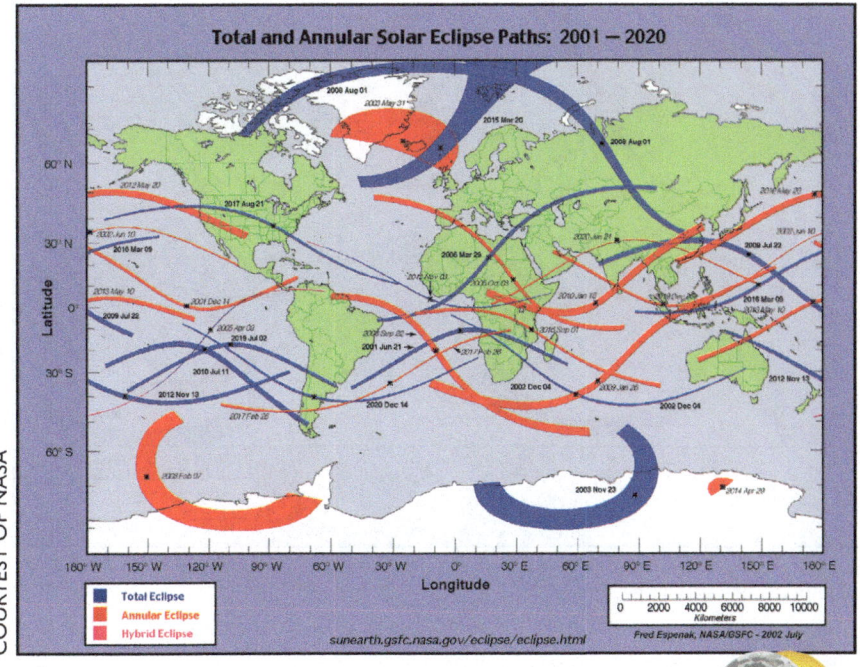

compare to the 2024 total eclipse. There is little in nature that equals the spectacle of the sun's corona and seeing stars in the day.

There will be multiple partial, annular, or hybrid eclipses across the world before the 2024 total eclipse. However many are in remote, inaccessible, or potentially dangerous locations on the globe. In 2019 and 2020, Chile and Argentina will experience total eclipses. The next total eclipse after that will occur over Antarctica in 2021. An extremely rare hybrid eclipse will happen in 2023 over the Indian Ocean, Australia, and Indonesia.

The next total solar eclipse viewable from the United States will occur on April 8, 2024. It will be visible in fifteen states: Texas, Oklahoma, Arkansas, Missouri, Kentucky, Illinois, Indiana, Ohio, Pennsylvania, New York, Vermont, New Hampshire, and Maine. A small corner of both Michigan and Tennessee will see the edge of the totality.

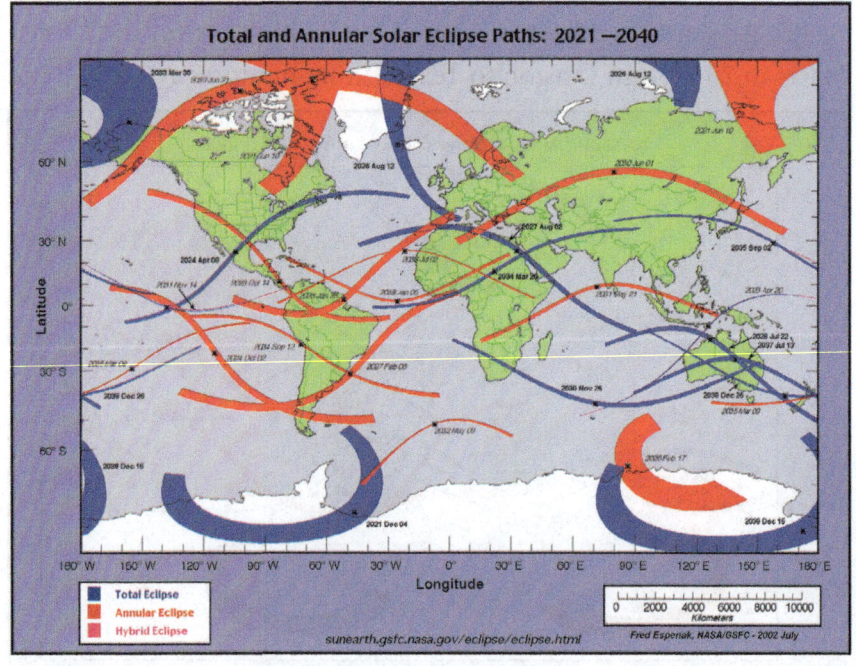

COURTESY OF NASA

Viewing and Photographing the Eclipse

AT-HOME PINHOLE METHOD

Use the pinhole method to view the eclipse safely. It costs little but is the safest technique there is. Take a stiff piece of single-layer cardboard and punch a clean pinhole. Let the sun shine through the pinhole onto another piece of cardboard. That's it!

Never look at the sun through the pinhole. Your back should be toward the sun to protect your eyes. To brighten the image, simply move the back piece of cardboard closer to the pinhole. To see it larger, move the back cardboard farther away. Do not make the pinhole larger. It will only distort the crescent sun.

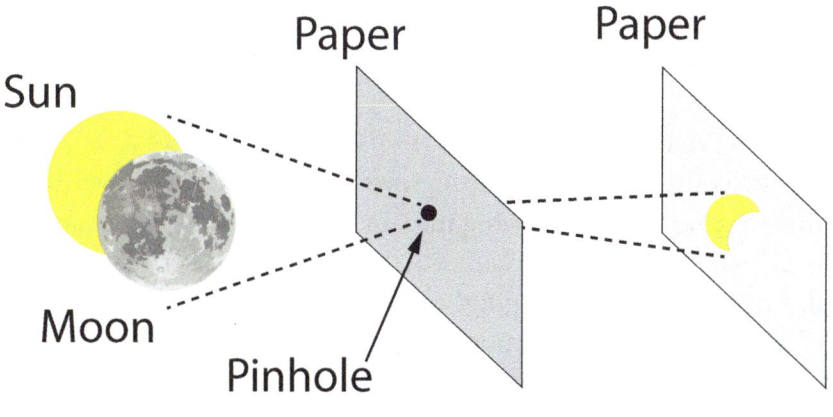

WELDING GOGGLES

Welding goggles that have a rating of fourteen or higher are another useful eclipse viewing tool. The goggles can be used to view the solar eclipse directly. Do not use the goggles to look through binoculars or telescopes, as the goggles could potentially shatter due to intense direct heat. Avoid long periods of gazing with the goggles. Look away every so often. Give your eyes a break.

SOLAR FILTERS FOR TELESCOPES

The ONLY safe way to view solar eclipses using telescopes or binoculars is to use solar filters. The filters are coated with metal to diminish the full intensity of the sun. Although the filters can be expensive, it is better to purchase a quality filter rather than an inexpensive one that could shatter or melt from the heat.

The filters attach to the front of the telescope for easy viewing. Remember to give your telescope cooling breaks. Rapid heating can damage your equipment with or without filters attached.

Watch Out for Unsafe Filters

There are several myths surrounding solar filters for eclipse viewing. In order for filters to be safe, they must be specially designed for looking at a solar eclipse. The following are all unsafe for eclipse viewing and can lead to retinal damage: developed colored or chromogenic film, black-and-white negatives such as X-rays, CDs with aluminum, smoked glass, floppy disk covers, black-and-white film with no silver, sunglasses, or polarizing films.

Watch Out for Unsafe Eclipse Glasses

During the 2017 total eclipse, several vendors sold eclipse glasses that were not safe for viewing the sun. Although they were marketed as safe and were even marked with the ISO 12312-2 certification, they did not block eye-damaging visible, infrared, and ultraviolet light. Check the American Astronomical Society's website (eclipse.aas.org) for a list of reputable eclipse glasses vendors.

Viewing with Binoculars

When viewing the eclipse with binoculars, it is important to use solar filters on both lenses until totality. Only then is it safe to remove the filter. As the sun becomes visible after totality, replace the filters for safe viewing. Protect your pupils. Remember to give your binoculars a cool-down break between viewings. They can overheat rapidly from being pointed directly at the sun even with filters attached.

Planning Ahead

There are many things to keep in mind when viewing a total eclipse. It is important to plan ahead to get the most out of this extraordinary experience.

Understanding Sun Position

All compass bearings in this book are true north. All compasses point to Earth's magnetic north. The difference between these two measurements is called magnetic declination. The magnetic declination for New York is:

13° 22' W ± 0° 22' (for Albany in 2020)

Adjust the declination from the azimuth bearing as given in the text, and set your compass to that direction.

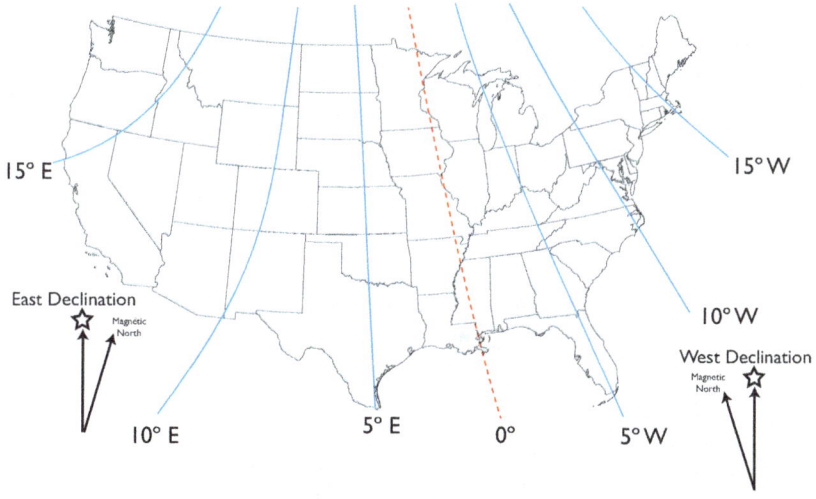

If you purchase a compass with a built-in declination adjustment, you can change the setting once and eliminate the calculations. The Suunto M-3G compass has this correction. A compass with a sighting mirror or wire will help you make a more accurate azimuth sighting.

The Suunto M-3G also has an inclinometer. This allows you to measure the elevation of any object above the horizon. Use this to figure out how high the sun will be above your position.

You can also use a smartphone inclinometer and compass for this purpose. Make sure to calibrate your smartphone's compass before every use, otherwise it might indicate the wrong bearing. Set the smartphone compass for true north to match the book. Understand the compass prior to April 8. There will be little time to guess or search on Google. Smartphone and GPS compasses are "sticky." Their compasses don't swing as freely as a magnetic compass does.

The author has used his magnetic compass for azimuth measurements and a smartphone to measure elevation. Combining these two tools will allow you to make the best sightings possible.

Outdoor sporting goods stores in most towns and cities carry compasses. Purchase and practice with a good compass in your hometown well before the event. Take the time to learn how to use it before the day of the eclipse. You do not want to struggle with orienteering basics under pressure.

Sun Azimuth

Azimuth is the compass angle along the horizon, with 0° corresponding to north, and increasing in a clockwise direction. 90° is east, 180° is south, and 270° is west.

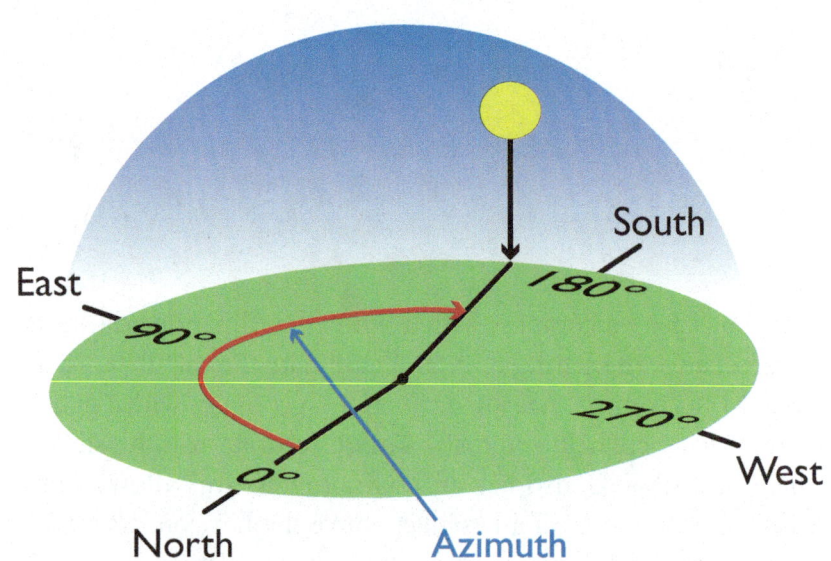

Sun Elevation

Altitude is the sun's angle up from the horizon. A 0° altitude means exactly on the horizon and 90° means "straight up."

Using the sun azimuth and elevation data, you can predict the position of the sun at any given time. Positions given in this book coincide with the time of eclipse totality unless otherwise noted.

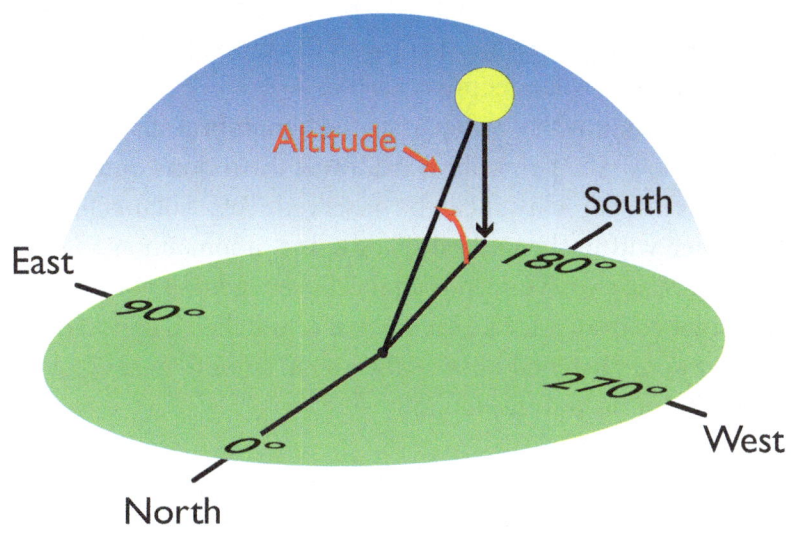

ECLIPSE DATA FOR SELECT NEW YORK LOCATIONS

LOCATION	TOTALITY START (EDT)	ALTITUDE	AZIMUTH
BUFFALO	3:18:16PM	45°	225°
JAMESTOWN	3:17:48PM	46°	225°
NIAGARA FALLS	3:18:15PM	45°	225°
ROCHESTER	3:20:02PM	44°	227°
SYRACUSE	3:22:56PM	43°	230°
WATERTOWN	3:22:28PM	42°	229°

ECLIPSE PHOTOGRAPHY

Photographing an eclipse is an exciting challenge, as the moon's shadow moves near 2,000MPH. There is an element of danger and the pressure of time. Looking at the unfiltered sun through a camera can permanently damage your vision and your camera. If you are unsure, just enjoy the eclipse with specially designed eclipse glasses. Keep a solar filter on your lens during the eclipse and remove for the duration of totality!

Partial Vs. Total Solar Eclipse

To successfully and safely photograph a partial and total eclipse, it is important to understand the difference between the two. A solar eclipse occurs when the moon is positioned between the sun and Earth. The region where the shadow of the moon falls upon Earth's surface is where a solar eclipse is visible.

The moon's shadow has two parts—the penumbral shadow and the umbral shadow. The penumbral shadow is the moon's outer shadow where partial solar eclipses can be observed. Total solar eclipses can only be seen within the umbral shadow, the moon's inner shadow.

You cannot say you've seen a total eclipse when all you saw was a partial solar eclipse. It is like saying you've watched a concert, but in reality, you only listened outside the arena. In both cases, you have missed the drama and the action.

Photographing A Partial And Total Solar Eclipse

Aside from the region where the outer shadow of the moon is cast, a partial solar eclipse is also visible before a total solar eclipse within

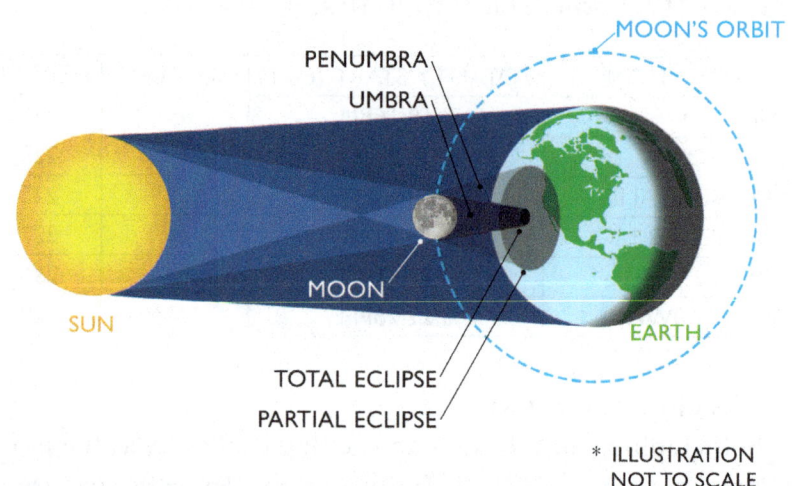

* ILLUSTRATION NOT TO SCALE

the inner shadow region. In both cases, it is imperative to use a solar filter on the lens for both photography and safety reasons. This is the only difference between taking a partial eclipse and a total eclipse photograph of the sun.

To photograph a total solar eclipse, you must be within the Path of Totality, the surface of the Earth within the moon's umbral shadow.

The Challenge

A total solar eclipse only lasts for a couple of minutes. It is brief, but the scenario it brings is unforgettable. Seeing the radiant sun slowly being covered by darkness gives the spectator a high level of anticipation and indescribable excitement. Once the moon completely covers the sun's radiance, the corona is finally visible. In the darkness, the sun's corona shines, capturing the crowd's full attention. Watching this phenomenon is a breathtaking experience.

Amidst all the noise, cheering, and excitement, you have no more than a few minutes to take a perfect photograph. The key to this is planning. You need to plan, practice, and perfect what you will do when the big moment arrives because there is no replay. The pressure is enormous. You only have a short time to capture the totality and the sun's corona using different exposures.

Plan, Practice, Perfect

It is important to practice photographing before the actual phenomenon arrives. Test your chosen imaging setup for flaws. Rehearse over and over until your body remembers what you will do from the moment you arrive at your chosen spot to the moment you pack up and leave the area.

You will discover potential problems regarding vibrations and focus that you can address immediately. This minimizes the variables that might affect your photographs at the most critical moment.

It's common for experienced eclipse chasers to lose track of what they plan to do. Write down what you expect to do. Practice it time and again. Play annoying, distracting music while you practice. Try photographing in the worst weather possible. Do anything you can to practice under pressure. Eclipse day is not the time to practice.

Once the sun is completely covered, don't just take photographs. Capture the experience and the image of the total solar eclipse in your mind as well. Set up cameras around you to record not just the total solar eclipse but also the excitement and reaction of the crowd.

Eclipse Photography Gear

What do you need to photograph the total eclipse? There are only a few pieces of equipment that you'll need. Preparing to photograph an eclipse successfully takes time. Not only do you have to be skilled and have the right gear, you have to be in the correct place.

Basic Eclipse Photography Equipment
- Solar viewing glasses (verify authenticity)
- Lens solar filter
- Minimum 300mm lens
- Stable tripod that can be tilted to 60° vertical
- High-resolution DSLR
- Spare batteries for everything
- Secondary camera to photograph people, the horizon, etc.
- Remote cable or wireless release

Additional Items
- Video camera
- Video camera tripod
- Quality pair of binoculars
- Solar filters for each binocular lens
- Photo editing software

Equipment to Prepare Before the Big Day

A. Solar viewing glasses
You need a pair of solar viewing glasses as the eclipse approaches.

B. Solar Filter
Partial and total eclipse photography is different from normal photography. Even if only 1% of the sun's surface is visible, it is still approximately 10,000 times brighter than the moon. Before totality, use a solar filter on your lens. Do not look at the sun with your eyes. It can cause irreparable damage to your retinas.

DO NOT leave your camera pointed at the sun without a solar filter attached. The sun will melt the inside of your camera. Think of a magnifying glass used to torch ants and multiply that by one hundred.

C. Lens

To capture the corona's majesty, you need to use a telescope or a telephoto lens. The best focal length, which will give you a large image of the sun's disk, is 400mm and above. You don't want to waste all your efforts by bringing home a small dot where the black disk and majestic corona are supposed to be.

D. Tripod

Bring a stable enough tripod to support your camera properly to avoid unsteady shots and repeated adjustments. Either will ruin your photos. It also needs to be portable in case you need to change locations for a better shot. *Shut off camera stabilization on a tripod!*

E. Camera

You need to remember to set your camera to its highest resolution to capture all the details. Set your camera to:

- 14-bit RAW is ideal, otherwise
- JPG, Fine compression, Maximum resolution

Bracket your exposures. Shoot at various shutter speeds to capture different brightnesses in the corona. Note that stopping your lens all the way down may not result in the sharpest images.

Choose the lowest possible ISO for the best quality while maintaining a high shutter speed to prevent blurred shots. Set your camera to manual. Do not use AUTO ISO. Your camera will be fooled. The night before, test the focus position of your lens using a bright star or the moon.

Constantly double-check your focus. Be paranoid about this. You can deal with a grainy picture. No amount of Photoshop will fix a blurry, out-of-focus picture.

F. Batteries

Remember to bring fresh batteries! Make sure that you have enough power to capture the most important moments. Swap in fresh batteries thirty minutes before totality.

G. Remote release

Use a wired or wireless remote release to fire the camera's shutter. This will reduce the amount of camera vibration.

H. Video Camera

Run a video camera of yourself. Capture all the things you say and do during the totality. You'll be amazed at your reaction.

I. Photo editing software

You will need quality photo editing software to process your eclipse images. Adobe Lightroom and Photoshop are excellent programs to extract the most out of your images. Become well versed in how to use them at least a month before the eclipse.

J. Smartphone applications

The following smartphone applications will aid in your photography planning: Wunderground, Skyview, Photographer's Ephemeris, Sunrise and Sunset Calculator, SunCalc, and Sun Surveyor among others.

CAMERA PHONES

Smartphone cameras are useful for many things but not eclipse photography. An iPhone 6 camera has a 63° horizontal field of view and is 3264 pixels across. If you attempt to photograph the eclipse, the sun will be a measly 30-40 pixels wide depending on the phone. Digital pinch zoom won't help here. If you want *National Geographic* images, you'll need a serious camera and lens, far beyond any smartphone.

Consider instead using a smartphone to run a time-lapse of the entire event. The sun will be minuscule when shot on a smartphone. Think of something else exciting and interesting do to with it. Purchase a Gorilla Pod, inexpensive tripod, or selfie stick and mount the smartphone somewhere unique.

Also, partial and total eclipse light is strange and ethereal. Consider using that light to take unique pictures of things and people. It's rare and you may have something no one else does.

Focal Length & the Size of Sun

The size of the sun in a photo depends on the lens focal length. A 300mm lens is the recommended minimum on a full-frame (FF) DSLR. Lenses up to this size are relatively inexpensive. For more magnification, use an APS-C (crop) size sensor. Cameras with these sensors provide an advantage by capturing a larger sun.

For the same focal length, an APS-C sensor will provide a greater apparent magnification of any object. As a consequence, a shorter, less expensive lens can be used to capture the same size sun.

The below figure shows the size of the sun on a camera sensor at various focal lengths. As can be seen with the 200mm lens, the sun is quite small. On a full-frame camera at 200mm, the sun will be 371 pixels wide on a Nikon D810, a 36-megapixel body. A lower resolution FF camera will result in an even smaller sun.

Printing a 24-inch image shot on a Nikon D810 with a 200mm lens at a standard 300 pixels per inch results in a small sun. On this size paper, the sun will be a miserly 1.25 inches wide!

Photographing the eclipse with a lens shorter than 300mm will leave you with little to work with. Using a 400mm lens and printing a 24-inch print will result in a 2.5-inch-wide sun. For as massive as the sun is, it is a challenge to take a large photograph of the sun. The sun will appear to move fast with a 500mm lens, too. Plan to adjust.

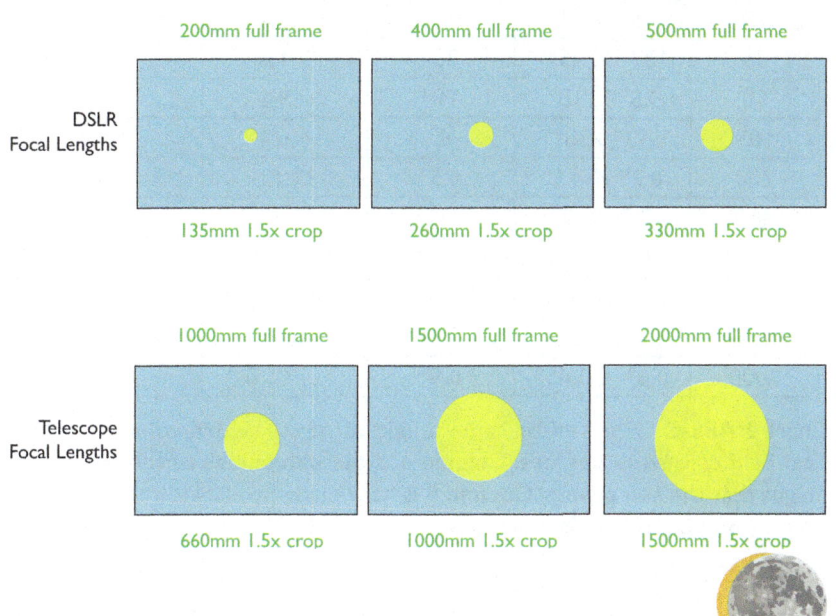

DSLR Focal Lengths

200mm full frame	400mm full frame	500mm full frame
135mm 1.5x crop	260mm 1.5x crop	330mm 1.5x crop

Telescope Focal Lengths

1000mm full frame	1500mm full frame	2000mm full frame
660mm 1.5x crop	1000mm 1.5x crop	1500mm 1.5x crop

FOCAL LENGTH	FOV FULL FRAME	FF VERT. ANGLE	% OF FF	SUN PIXEL SIZE
14	104° X 81°	81°	0.7%	32.1
20	84° X 62°	62°	0.9%	41.9
28	65° X 46°	46°	1.2%	56.5
35	54° X 38°	38°	1.4%	68.5
50	40° X 27°	27°	2.0%	96.4
105	19° X 13°	13°	4.1%	200.2
200	10° X 7°	7°	7.6%	371.9
400	5° X 3.4°	3.4°	15.6%	765.6
500	4° X 2.7°	2.7°	19.6%	964.2
1000	2° X 1.3°	1.3°	40.8%	2002.5
1500	1.4° X 0.9°	0.9°	58.9%	2892.6
2000	1° X 0.68°	0.68°	77.9%	3828.4

Chart 1: Full-frame camera field of view. The 3rd column is the vertical field of view in degrees. Column 4 is the percentage of the total sensor height that the sun covers. Column 5 is how many pixels wide the sun will be on a 36MP Nikon D810. (Values are estimates)

FOCAL LENGTH	FOV CROP	CROP VERT DEG	% OF CROP	SUN PIXEL SIZE
14	80° X 58°	58°	0.9%	33.9
20	61° X 43°	43°	1.2%	45.8
28	45° X 31°	31°	1.7%	63.5
35	37° X 25°	25°	2.1%	78.7
50	26° X 18°	18°	2.9%	109.3
105	13° X 8°	8°	6.6%	245.9
200	6.7° X 4.5°	4.5°	11.8%	437.2
400	3.4° X 2°	2°	26.5%	983.7
500	2.7° X 1.8	1.8°	29.4%	1093.0
1000	1.3° X 0.9°	0.9°	58.9%	2186.0
1500	0.9° X 0.6°	0.6°	88.3%	3278.9
2000	0.6° X 0.45°	0.5°	117.8%	4371.9

Chart 2: APS-C Crop sensor camera field of view. The 3rd column is the vertical field of view in degrees. Column 4 is the percentage of the total sensor height that the sun covers. Column 5 is how many pixels wide the sun will be on a 12mp Nikon D300s. (Values are estimates)

The big challenge is the cost of the lens. Lenses longer than 300mm are expensive. They also require heavier tripods and specialized tripod heads. The 70-300mm lenses from Nikon, Canon, Tamron, and others are relatively affordable options. It is worth spending time at a local camera shop to try different lenses. Long focal-length lenses are a significant investment, especially for a single event.

To achieve a large eclipse image, you will need a long focal-length lens, ideally at least 400mm. A standard 70-300mm lens set to 300mm will show a small sun. At 500mm, the sun image becomes larger and covers more of the sensor area. The corona will take up a significant portion of the frame. By 1000mm, the corona will exceed the capture area on a full-frame sensor. See the picture in this chapter for sun size simulations for different focal lengths.

Suggested Exposures

To photograph the partial eclipse, the camera must have a solar filter attached. If not, the intense light from the sun may damage (fry) the inside of your camera. This has happened to the author. The exposure depends on the density (darkness) of the solar filter used.

As a starting point, set the camera to ISO 100, f/8, and with the solar filter on, try an exposure of 1/2000. Make adjustments based on the filter used, histogram, and highlight warning.

Turn on the highlight warning in your camera. This feature is commonly called "blinkies." This warning will help you detect if the image is overexposed or not.

Once the Baily's Beads, prominences, and corona become visible, there will only be a few minutes to take bracketed shots. It will take at least eleven shots to capture the various areas of the sun's corona and stars. The brightness varies considerably. No commercially available camera can capture the incredible dynamic range of the different portions of the delicate corona. This requires taking multiple photographs and digitally combining them afterward.

During totality, try these exposure times at ISO 100 and f/8: 1/4000, 1/2000, 1/1000, 1/250, 1/60, 1/30, 1/15, 1/4, 1/2, 1 sec, and 4 sec.

Disable camera/lens stabilization on a tripod!

Photography Time

Set the camera to full-stop adjustments. It will reduce the time spent fiddling. As an example, the author tried the above shot sequence, adjusting the shutter speed as fast as possible.

It took thirty-three seconds to shoot the above 11 shots using 1/3-stop increments. This was without adjusting composition, focus, or anything else but the shutter speed. When the camera was set to full stop increments, it only took twenty-two seconds to step through the same shutter speed sequence. Use a remote release to reduce camera shake.

Assuming the totality lasts less than two minutes, only four shot sequences could be made using 1/3-stop increments. Yet six shot sequences could be made when the camera was set to full stop steps. Zero time was spent looking at the back LCD to analyze highlights and the histogram.

Now add in the bare minimum time to check the highlight warning. It took sixty-three seconds to shoot and check each image using full stops. And that was without changing the composition to allow for sun movement, bumping the tripod, etc. Looking at the LCD ("chimping") consumed **half** of the totality time.

This test was done in the comfort of home under no pressure. In real world conditions, it may be possible to successfully shoot only one sequence. If you plan to capture the entire dynamic range of the totality, you must practice the sequence until you have it down cold. If you normally fumble with your camera, do not underestimate the difficulty, frustration, and stress of total eclipse photography.

Most importantly, trying to shoot this sequence allowed for zero time to simply look at the totality to enjoy the spectacle.

Avoid Last Minute Purchases

You should purchase whatever you think you'll need to photograph the eclipse early. This event will be nothing short of massive. Remember the hot toy of the year? Multiply that frenzy by a thousand. Everyone will want to try to capture their own photo.

Do not wait until the last few weeks before the eclipse to purchase cameras, lenses, filters, tripods, viewing glasses, and associated material. Consider that the totality of the eclipse will streak across

America. Everyone who wants to photograph the eclipse will order at the same time. If you wait until too late to buy what you need, it's conceivable that solar filters to create a total eclipse photo will be sold out in the United States. All filters sold out during the 2017 total eclipse. Whether this happens or not, do not wait to make your purchases. It may be too late.

Practice

You will need to practice with your equipment. Things may go wrong that you don't anticipate. If you've never photographed a partial or total eclipse, taking quality shots is more difficult than you think. Practice shooting the sequence with a midday sun. This will tell you if you have your exposures and timing correct. Figure out what you need well in advance.

Practice photographing the full moon and stars at night. Capture the moon in full daylight to learn how your camera reacts. Astrophotography is challenging and requires practice.

The August 21, 2017, eclipse as seen in Jackson, WY, shot with a Nikon D800 with an 80-400mm lens set to 340mm. The sun is 644 pixels wide on the 7360x4912 image.

This image is shown straight out of the camera without modification. Even with a high-quality camera and lens, photographing an eclipse is a challenge.

42 ◉ New York Total Eclipse Guide 2024

Total eclipse position

Sun's path from sunrise

LOCATIONS

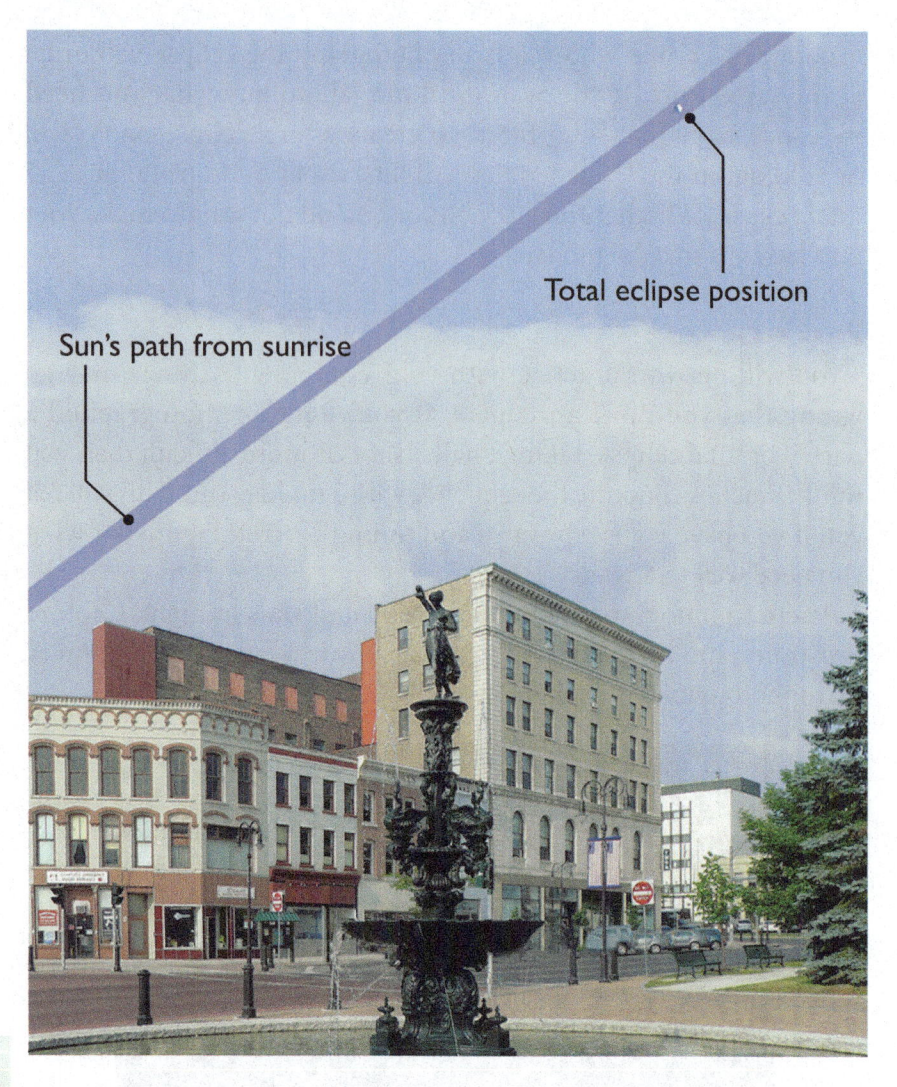

The eclipse will follow this approximate path on the afternoon of April 8, 2024 in Watertown, NY. Hopefully it won't be this cloudy on the day of the eclipse.

Note that this image is a simulation and approximation the sun's path and where the total eclipse may appear from one perspective. Refer to the eclipse position data for a more accurate location.

◉ is the symbol for the sun and first appeared in Europe during the Renaissance.
☾ is the ancient symbol for the moon.

Viewing Locations Around New York

Millions of people will travel to and around New York to view the total eclipse. There are few obstructions and there is a vast amount of space to view the total eclipse from.

If the weather is questionable, seek out a new location as soon as possible. If you wait until the hour before the eclipse, you may find yourself stuck in traffic, as others will be looking for a viewing location. Be safe on the roadways, as drivers may be distracted.

This section contains popular, alternative, and little-known locations to watch the eclipse. As long as there are no clouds or smoke from fires, the partial eclipse will be viewable from anywhere in the state. Niagara Falls will be a memorable total eclipse location.

Suggested Total Eclipse View Points

Towns and Cities

- Buffalo
- Canton
- Childwold
- Fredonia
- Harrisville
- Jamestown
- Malone
- Massena
- Oswego
- Plattsburg
- Potsdam
- Rochester
- Syracuse
- Watertown

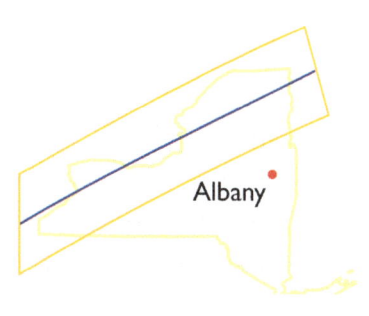

New York Total Eclipse Path

Unique Locations

- Adirondack State Park
- Five Ponds Wilderness
- Niagara Falls
- Lake Champlain
- Lake Erie
- Lake Ontario

Buffalo

Elevation: 600 feet
Population: 256,000
Main road/hwy: Multiple

Overview

Buffalo is the second largest city in the state of New York. The city is rich in history and culture. Buffalo serves as the seat of Erie County and is a remarkable gateway for travel and commerce at the Canada-US border. The rich history of Buffalo is in part because it was inhabited in the seventeenth century by the Iroquois tribe and then later by French settlers. The city saw a tremendous boom in the nineteenth and twentieth centuries and today is considered to be a wonderful tourist destination, complete with great access to Lake Erie, Niagara River, and an extensive system of parks designed by Frederick Law Olmsted.

Getting There

Buffalo is a major city in New York connected by multiple highways and is served by multiple airline companies.

Totality Duration

3 minutes 45 seconds

Notes

Visit the city's website for eclipse updates at www.ci.buffalo.ny.us.

Event	Time (EDT)	Altitude	Azimuth
Sunrise	6:44:00AM	0°	78°
Eclipse Start	2:04:52PM	53°	200°
Totality Start	3:18:16PM	45°	225°
Totality End	3:22:01PM	45°	227°
Eclipse End	4:32:05PM	34°	245°
Sunset	7:50:00PM	0°	281°

Canton

Elevation: 377 feet
Population: 6,524
Main road/hwy: US 11

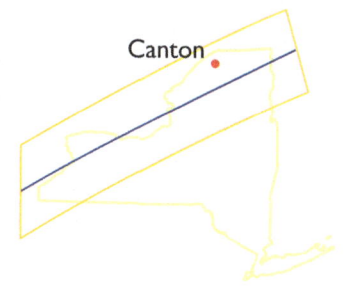

Overview

Located in stunning St. Lawrence County, Canton has a population of over six thousand and is comprised of two different villages. While one of these villages is named Canton, the other is called Rensselaer Falls.

Named after the great port of Canton in China, the town is home to St. Lawrence University and SUNY Canton. The Brick Chapel Church and Cemetery of Canton were listed on the National Register of Historic Places in 2005. Interested in viewing the 2024 eclipse from here? Canton is a wonderful place to do it, thanks to its elevation and northern location but make sure to keep your eye on the weather forecast.

Getting There

Drive northwest on US 11 from Watertown for fifty-nine miles to reach Canton.

Totality Duration

3 minutes 12 seconds

Notes

The Canton city website will have updates at cantonny.gov.

Event	Time (EDT)	Altitude	Azimuth
Sunrise	6:27:00AM	0°	78°
Eclipse Start	2:11:32PM	50°	207°
Totality Start	3:23:46PM	41°	230°
Totality End	3:26:58PM	41°	231°
Eclipse End	4:35:52PM	31°	248°
Sunset	7:37:00PM	0°	281°

Childwold

Elevation: 1,627 feet
Population: 36
Main road/hwy: NY 3

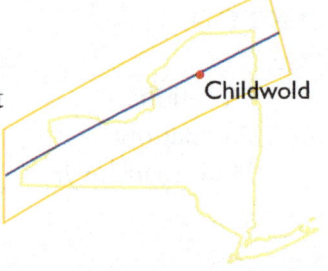

Overview

Childwold is one of the best-kept secrets in New York. This small, one-of-a-kind community is part of Adirondack Park, made up of over one hundred unique towns, villages, and hamlets. Childwold is located on the western side of the Town of Piercefield, and this remarkable hamlet has a population of less than one hundred! Folks drive through this small community at one time or another, and most don't realize that it's really worth slowing down and seeing the sites. This is no bustling metropolis, but it's a wonderful place to spend the afternoon and is a remarkable viewing spot for the 2024 eclipse. Why not take a trip here to see if it will work for your eclipse plans?

Getting There

Drive northeast from Watertown on NY 3 for sixty-two miles to reach the town of Childwold.

Totality Duration

3 minutes 35 seconds

Notes

www.tupperlake.com/blog/2015/10/destination-childwold

Event	Time (EDT)	Altitude	Azimuth
Sunrise	6:26:00AM	0°	78°
Eclipse Start	2:12:00PM	50°	208°
Totality Start	3:24:06PM	41°	231°
Totality End	3:27:41PM	41°	232°
Eclipse End	4:36:01PM	30°	248°
Sunset	7:35:00PM	0°	281°

Fredonia

Elevation:	722 feet
Population:	10,639
Main road/hwy:	I-90

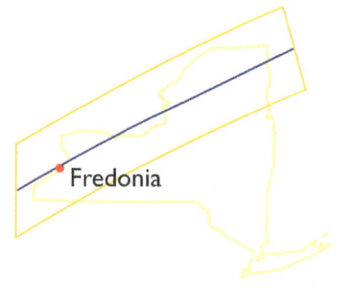

Overview

Located in stunning Chautauqua County, Fredonia is a destination that you'll not soon forget. With a population of just over ten thousand, Fredonia is located in the town of Pomfret south of Lake Erie. Bordering on the city of Dunkirk, the village is home to the State University of New York at Fredonia. The town was incorporated in 1829, and its original name was Canadaway, meaning "among the hemlocks." Fredonia was coined by Samuel Latham Mitchell, coupling the word "freedom" with a Latin ending. Today Fredonia boasts of a number of historical attractions as well as a brimming university culture.

Getting There

Drive from Buffalo on I-90 south and then southwest for forty-nine miles to reach Fredonia.

Totality Duration

3 minutes 40 seconds

Notes

Visit Fredonia's website at villageoffredoniany.com for eclipse updates in late 2023.

Event	Time (EDT)	Altitude	Azimuth
Sunrise	v	0°	79°
Eclipse Start	2:03:44PM	53°	199°
Totality Start	3:17:27PM	46°	225°
Totality End	3:21:08PM	46°	226°
Eclipse End	4:31:33PM	35°	244°
Sunset	7:51:00PM	0°	281°

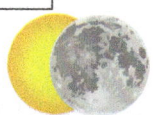

Harrisville

Elevation:	807 feet
Population:	619
Main road/hwy:	NY 3

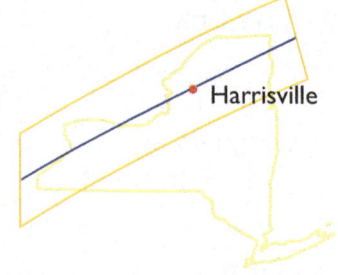

Overview

Located in Lewis County, this charming New York village has a population that is just under a thousand. It is part of the Town of Diana in south Ogdensburg. Harrisville is an ideal location to spot the 2024 eclipse because of its northern location. New York Route 812 and New York Route 3 pass through the town, making it very easy to access. With a number of historical sites and a culture steeped in hospitality, Harrisville makes for a great weekend getaway, and many find that when they come here, they never wish to leave.

Getting There

Drive east from Watertown on NY 3 for thirty-four miles to reach the hamlet of Harrisville.

Totality Duration

3 minutes 37 seconds

Notes

Harrisville's website will have eclipse updates and ideas where to stay and view at villageofharrisvilleny.org.

Event	Time (EDT)	Altitude	Azimuth
Sunrise	6:29:00AM	0°	78°
Eclipse Start	2:10:59PM	50°	207°
Totality Start	3:23:15PM	42°	230°
Totality End	3:26:53PM	41°	231°
Eclipse End	4:35:26PM	41°	231°
Sunset	7:37:00PM	0°	281°

Jamestown

Elevation:	1,378 feet
Population:	29,775
Main road/hwy:	I-86

Overview

Travelers flock to Jamestown for a number of reasons. There's so much that the city has to offer, such as excellent schools, abundant art, and performance opportunities, as well as friendly neighborhoods and warm hospitality. Whether you're just visiting or you choose to make Jamestown your home, you can enjoy the nearby ski resorts, nature preserves, golf courses, and so much more. Affordable homes and plenty of opportunities for entertainment and culture abound. Also, enjoy the bars, theater, and urban core that makes Jamestown stand out from the rest.

Getting There

Drive south then southwest from Buffalo on I-90 for thirty-five miles, then turn south on NY 60 and drive twenty-two miles to reach Jamestown.

Totality Duration

2 minutes 52 seconds

Notes

The Jamestown website, www.jamestownupclose.com, will have eclipse updates in 2024.

Event	Time (EDT)	Altitude	Azimuth
Sunrise	6:46:00AM	0°	79°
Eclipse Start	2:03:32PM	54°	199°
Totality Start	3:17:48PM	46°	225°
Totality End	3:20:40PM	46°	226°
Eclipse End	4:31:36PM	35°	245°
Sunset	7:51:00PM	0°	281°

Malone

Elevation: 790 feet
Population: 14,545
Main road/hwy: NY 11

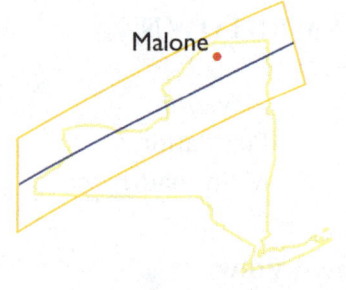

Overview

Malone offers you an experience that is purely New York. At the heart of northern New York County, the town is within the rolling fields between Canada and the Adirondacks. Its inhabitants, thanks to the abounding shops, activities, farms, and gorgeous lodging options, treasure this region. Be sure to visit the Adirondack Trail Scenic Byway, with 188 unforgettable miles of roads that twist and turn through the stunning Adirondacks. Do you love to ski? You've definitely come to the right place. Malone is picturesque during the winter, and downhill skiing is a must.

Getting There

Drive northeast from Watertown on US 11 for seventy miles, then turn east on NY 11 and drive for another thirty-six miles to reach Malone.

Totality Duration

3 minutes 14 seconds

Notes

Malone's town website will be a good starting point for any plans in the town: www.visitmalone.com.

Event	Time (EDT)	Altitude	Azimuth
Sunrise	6:24:00AM	0°	78°
Eclipse Start	2:12:55PM	49°	209°
Totality Start	3:24:51PM	41°	231°
Totality End	3:28:05PM	40°	232°
Eclipse End	4:36:16PM	30°	248°
Sunset	7:34:00PM	0°	281°

Massena

Elevation: 295 feet
Population: 12,883
Main road/hwy: NY 37

Overview

Looking for rich history in northern New York? Massena is a town in St. Lawrence County. It's located along the northern border of the country, and it's just south of the St. Lawrence River and the Canada-US border. With a population of just over twelve thousand, you'll find that the folks here are cultured, favor hospitality, and are quite proud of their town. This was one of the first towns settled in St. Lawrence County, and its rich history can be spotted at every turn. It was named after Andre Massena, a general and Marshal to Napoleon during the Napoleonic Wars.

Getting There

Drive north from Watertown on I-81 for fourteen miles, then turn right onto NY 411 for three miles, then continue on NY 37 for seventy-five miles to reach Massena.

Totality Duration

2 minutes 25 seconds

Notes

Point your web browser to massena.us to visit the Massena government website for eclipse lodging and event information.

Event	Time (EDT)	Altitude	Azimuth
Sunrise	6:26:00AM	0°	78°
Eclipse Start	2:12:10PM	49°	207°
Totality Start	3:24:35PM	41°	230°
Totality End	3:27:00PM	41°	231°
Eclipse End	4:35:44PM	30°	248°
Sunset	7:36:00PM	0°	281°

Oswego

Elevation: 285 feet
Population: 17,599
Main road/hwy: NY 481

Overview

The city of Oswego is home to a specular community of folks that take great pride in their history and their legacy. This city has enjoyed a real resurgence lately, with a thriving downtown buoyancy, complete with new restaurants, small businesses, and a lively ambience that visitors and residents take pride in. There are a number of events throughout the summer in Oswego that draw a huge crowd, and be sure to visit the weekly downtown Farmer's Market for crops that are as fresh as can be. No trip is complete without going to the Oswego Speedway and Fort Ontario.

Getting There

Drive north from Syracuse on NY 481 for thirty-nine miles to reach Oswego.

Totality Duration

3 minutes 30 seconds

Notes

Check the Oswego city website for eclipse event updates at www.oswegony.org.

Event	Time (EDT)	Altitude	Azimuth
Sunrise	6:34:00AM	0°	78°
Eclipse Start	2:08:44PM	51°	204°
Totality Start	3:21:37PM	43°	229°
Totality End	3:25:07PM	43°	230°
Eclipse End	4:34:22PM	32°	247°
Sunset	7:41:00PM	0°	281°

Viewing Locations ☾ 53

Plattsburgh

Elevation:	600 feet
Population:	256,000
Main road/hwy:	I-87

Overview

The City of Plattsburgh is idyllically located on Lake Champlain, in the northeast portion of New York State. Just twenty miles from the Canadian border, Plattsburgh sits on 6.1 million acres of land in what's known as Adirondack Park. Here you will find the famous Adirondack Mountains, with over one hundred summits that reach up to five thousand feet high. Plattsburgh is all about its people, and it was founded by Zephaniah Platt in 1785. Its northern location makes it ideal for the 2024 eclipse. Plan ahead! And be sure to not miss the Mayor's Cup Festival Regatta.

Getting There

Drive northeast from Watertown on US 11 for one hundred and eight miles, and then continue east on County Road 24 and NY 190 for forty-four miles to reach Plattsburg.

Totality Duration

3 minutes 33 seconds

Notes

Browse the city's website at www.cityofplattsburgh.com for eclipse event and safety updates.

Event	Time (EDT)	Altitude	Azimuth
Sunrise	6:20:00AM	0°	78°
Eclipse Start	2:13:57PM	49°	210°
Totality Start	3:25:38PM	40°	232°
Totality End	3:29:11PM	40°	233°
Eclipse End	4:37:00PM	29°	249°
Sunset	7:30:00PM	0°	281°

Potsdam

Elevation: 433 feet
Population: 15,741
Main road/hwy: US 11

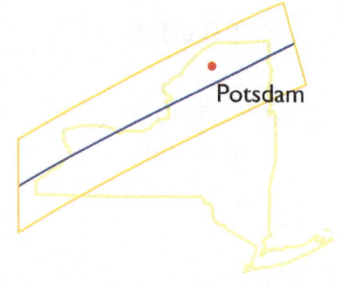

Overview

The lovely town of Potsdam is situated in the Adirondack foothills, just in the center of St. Lawrence County. There are two villages in Potsdam, including the Village of Potsdam and the Village of Norwood. Considered a cultural and educational center, the town is rich in technology, education, and art. Home to State University of Potsdam as well as the Clarkson University, the town has a youthful, vibrant energy, with a great emphasis on education, culture, and progress. Established in 1806, here is yet another ideal location in New York to see the upcoming eclipse. The accommodations are affordable, and all residents greet you with a smile.

Getting There

Drive northeast from Watertown on US 11 for seventy miles to reach the city of Potsdam.

Totality Duration

3 minutes 10 seconds

Notes

Visit the official Potsdam website at potsdamny.us for eclipse event information.

Event	Time (EDT)	Altitude	Azimuth
Sunrise	v	0°	78°
Eclipse Start	2:11:51PM	49°	207°
Totality Start	3:24:02PM	41°	230°
Totality End	3:27:12PM	41°	231°
Eclipse End	4:35:41PM	30°	248°
Sunset	7:36:00PM	0°	281°

Rochester

Elevation: 505 feet
Population: 208,880
Main road/hwy: I-490

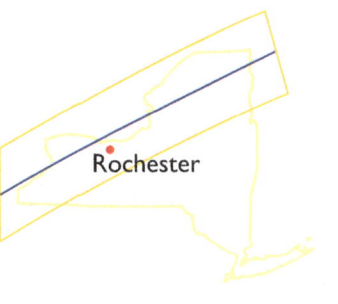

Overview

Rochester, New York, is so steeped in history that many people don't even stop to consider it! With remarkable attractions, museums, live theater, fine dining, and so much more, any trip to Rochester for the eclipse is one that you'll never forget. Rochester, the seat of Monroe County, is located on the southern shore of Lake Ontario in western New York and boasts a large population. It's the third most populous city in the state of New York. It was one of America's first boomtowns. If the weather is good, the skyline and landscape of Rochester should make for some excellent eclipse photographs.

Getting There

Rochester is a major city in New York. Multiple interstates and airline companies connect to the city.

Totality Duration

3 minutes 39 seconds

Notes

Rochester's official website will have eclipse updates at www.cityofrochester.gov.

Event	Time (EDT)	Altitude	Azimuth
Sunrise	6:39:00AM	0°	78°
Eclipse Start	2:06:54PM	52°	202°
Totality Start	3:20:02PM	44°	227°
Totality End	3:23:41PM	44°	228°
Eclipse End	4:33:19PM	33°	246°
Sunset	7:45:00PM	0°	282°

Syracuse

Elevation: 380 feet
Population: 143,378
Main road/hwy: Multiple

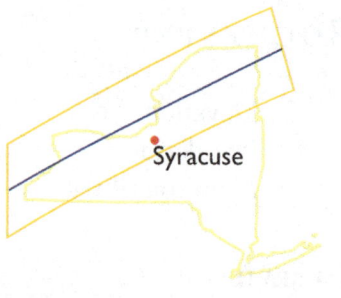

Overview

What could be more New York than Syracuse? This is the seat of Onondaga County, and it's the fifth most populous city in New York State. With a large population, Syracuse is the economic and educational hub of Central New York. The downtown convention complex makes Syracuse a top destination for businesses and commercial events. Named after a famous Greek city off the coast of Sicily, today Syracuse can be found at the intersection of Interstates 81 and 90. Be sure to visit Syracuse University, as well as Le-Moyne College. Both universities will have eclipse-related activities.

Getting There

Syracuse is served by multiple freeways and airline companies, as it is a major city in New York.

Totality Duration

1 minute 28 seconds

Notes

Point your browser to the official Syracuse website at www.syrgov.net for eclipse updates. Note that Syracuse is near the edge of the eclipse and will not be under totality as long as other locations.

Event	Time (EDT)	Altitude	Azimuth
Sunrise	6:33:00AM	0°	79°
Eclipse Start	2:08:55PM	52°	205°
Totality Start	3:22:56PM	43°	230°
Totality End	3:24:24PM	43°	230°
Eclipse End	4:34:42PM	32°	247°
Sunset	7:39:00PM	0°	281°

Watertown

Elevation:	466 feet
Population:	25,900
Main road/hwy:	I-81

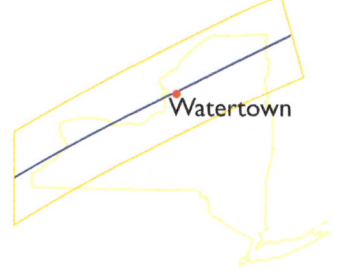

Overview

Thinking about visiting Watertown for the 2024 eclipse? You've made a great choice. Here you'll find a sprawling town located seventy miles north of Syracuse and thirty miles south of Canada. It's directly under the centerline of the eclipse. This little city was settled in 1800 and carries a two-hundred-year legacy that you can still enjoy today. Originally settled by New England pioneers, today you'll still find the pioneering spirit instilled in its people. Nearby, find the mighty Black River, and be sure to visit the historic Public Square. Whether you're an outdoorsman or not, there's something for everyone in picturesque Watertown. Make your way to Lake Ontario for the best hiking, boating, fishing, camping, rafting, and so much more.

Getting There

Drive north from Syracuse on I-18 for seventy miles to reach the city of Watertown.

Totality Duration

3 minutes 38 seconds

Notes

Watertown's official website is www.watertown-ny.gov.

Event	Time (EDT)	Altitude	Azimuth
Sunrise	6:31:00AM	0°	78°
Eclipse Start	2:10:01PM	51°	206°
Totality Start	3:22:28PM	42°	229°
Totality End	3:26:07PM	42°	230°
Eclipse End	4:34:55PM	31°	247°
Sunset	7:39:00PM	0°	281°

Adirondack State Park

Elevation: Varies
Main road/hwy: Multiple

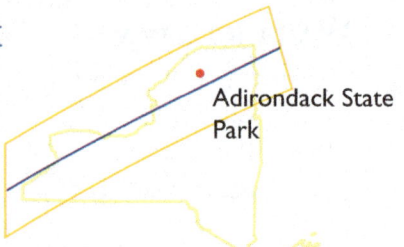

Overview

Do you want to know the secret for being in the right place to spot the 2024 eclipse? Go to the Adirondacks. The park was created in 1892 by the State of New York, and it boasts a diverse mountain landscape with pristine waterways, mountain peaks reaching toward the sky, and stunning boreal forests. The Adirondack Forest Preserve was established to protect this region. Everyone enjoys the remarkable preservation today. Take stock in the publicly protected area, and visit one of over one hundred towns and villages contained inside and around the park.

Getting There

The park area is large, covering over nine thousand square miles in northeast New York.

Totality Duration

3 minutes 2 seconds (for Long Lake)

Notes

Learn more about the park at visitadirondacks.com/about/adirondack-park.

Eclipse times are for Long Lake, NY.

Event	Time (EDT)	Altitude	Azimuth
Sunrise	6:25:00AM	0°	78°
Eclipse Start	2:12:06PM	50°	209°
Totality Start	3:24:34PM	41°	232°
Totality End	3:27:37PM	41°	232°
Eclipse End	4:36:15PM	30°	249°
Sunset	7:33:00PM	0°	281°

Five Ponds Wilderness

Elevation: Varies
Main road/hwy: Multiple

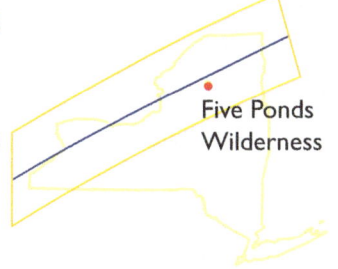

Overview

Looking for adventure? You've definitely come to the right place. Five Ponds Wilderness is open year-round, and admission is absolutely free to all. This sprawling 107,230-acre wilderness area combines with Pepperbox Wilderness as part of the Adirondack Forest Preserve. This is some of the remotest wilderness that you can find in New York State, and it offers some of the most exciting and entertaining outdoor activities. Go for a hike, have a picnic, or ride your bike on one of the countless trails that you'll find within the park. Winter is also a great time for cross-country skiing too.

Getting There

Drive east from Watertown on NY 3 for sixty miles and then turn south on County Road 61 for one mile to reach Wanakena and the edge of the wilderness area.

Totality Duration

3 minutes 34 seconds

Notes

Visit the New York website on the wilderness area at www.dec.ny.gov/lands/34719.html.

Event	Time (EDT)	Altitude	Azimuth
Sunrise	6:27:00AM	0°	80°
Eclipse Start	2:11:31PM	50°	208°
Totality Start	3:23:45PM	42°	231°
Totality End	3:27:19PM	41°	232°
Eclipse End	4:35:47PM	30°	248°
Sunset	7:35:00PM	0°	279°

Niagara Falls

Elevation: 614 feet
Main road/hwy: US 62

Overview

This might be the most sensational spot in the country to witness the total eclipse. It can be viewed directly over the Horseshoe Falls from Terrapin Point and Hurricane Deck at the Cave of the Winds. A wide angle lens will be needed to capture the eclipse and the waterfall together. From the Niagara Falls observation tower, the eclipse will be just to the right of the falls. The eclipse will be above the Rainbow Bridge from the park at the Niagara Gorge Discovery Center. Contact the Maid of the Mist boat tour for possible early-season rides for the eclipse. Make your reservations a year in advance if possible for hotels, tours, or rides. Note that travel between Canada and the United States may be difficult on the day before and of the eclipse, as there will be thousands of people vying for the best spot to view the totality in the afternoon near the falls.

Totality Duration

3 minutes 30 seconds

Notes

Visit the Niagara Falls park website at www.niagarafallsstatepark.com for more information about the above attractions.

Event	Time (EDT)	Altitude	Azimuth
Sunrise	6:45:00AM	0°	79°
Eclipse Start	2:04:48PM	53°	199°
Totality Start	3:18:15PM	45°	225°
Totality End	3:21:46PM	45°	226°
Eclipse End	4:31:54PM	34°	244°
Sunset	7:51:00PM	0°	281°

Viewing Locations « 61

The total eclipse over Niagara Falls

270° West

225°

Sun azimuth diagram (not to scale)

Rainbow Bridge

Niagara Falls State Park

American Falls

Bridal Veil Falls

Green Island

Niagara River

Goat Island

Horseshoe Falls

Eclipse Location

United States
Canada

LOCATIONS

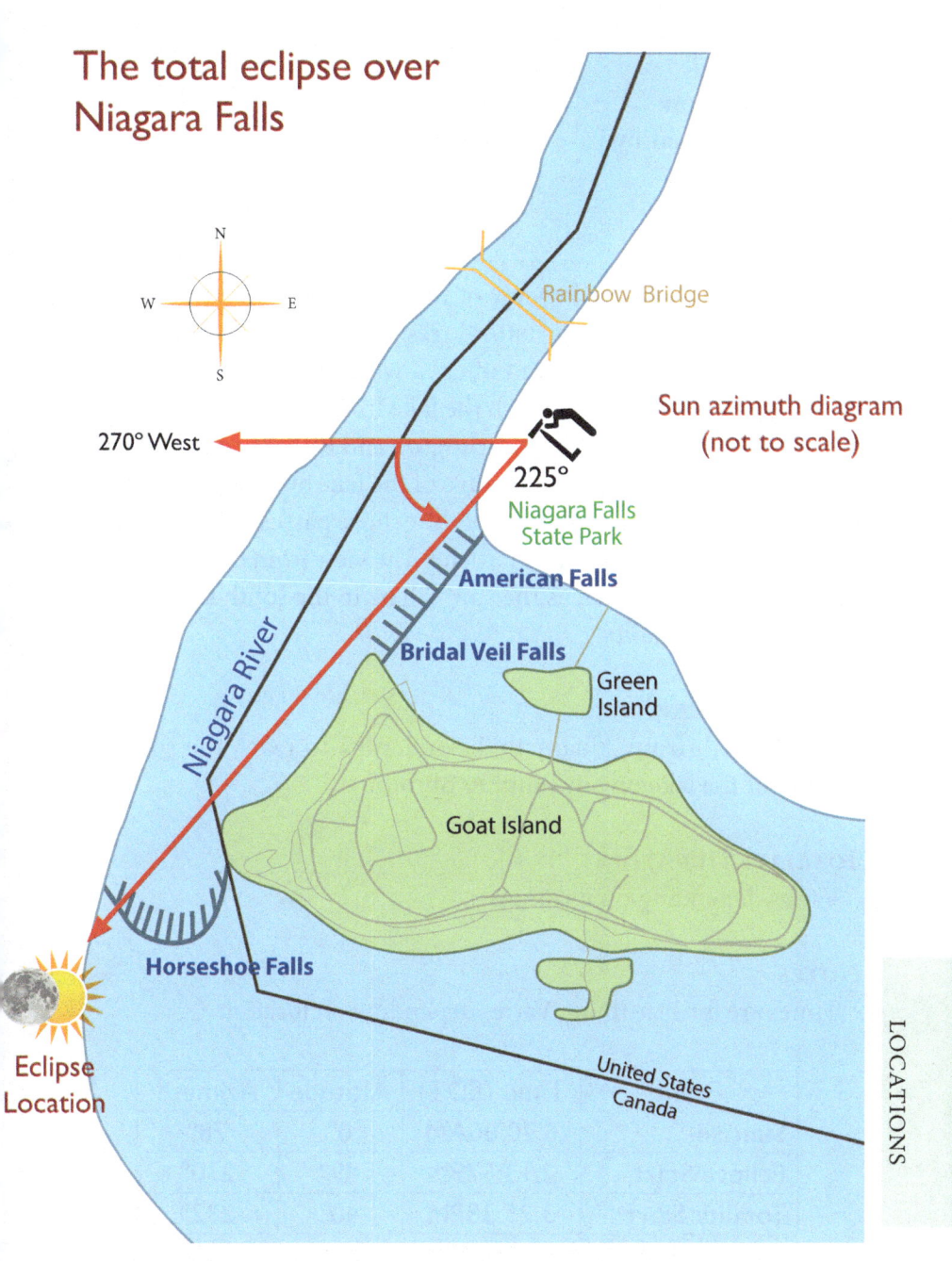

The eclipse can be seen over Horseshoe Falls along several locations on the American side of the Niagara River.

Lake Champlain

Elevation: 98 feet
Main road/hwy: US 167

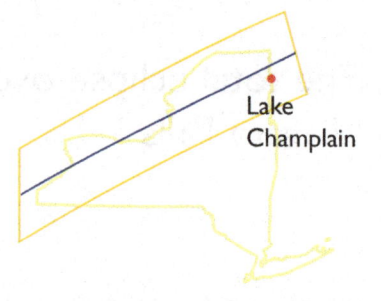

Overview

When looking for a lake view of the eclipse, there's nothing quite like Lake Champlain. This natural freshwater lake is located in Vermont as well as New York and offers a whole host of remarkable activities and sights. You can reach the lake from multiple cities in New York and Vermont, including Burlington and Plattsburgh. The city of Ticonderoga is on the southern edge of the lake but is just outside the total eclipse area. The centerline of the eclipse passes only a few miles north of Plattsburg at Point Au Roche. The view from the eastern side of the lake will be better, as the sun will be in the south to southwest sky during the totality.

Getting There

Drive north from Albany to Ticonderoga to reach the southern section of the lake on any number of routes.

Totality Duration

Varies depending on location.

Notes

Times are for Plattsburg. Varies depending on location.

Event	Time (EDT)	Altitude	Azimuth
Sunrise	6:20:00AM	0°	78°
Eclipse Start	2:13:57PM	49°	210°
Totality Start	3:25:38PM	40°	232°
Totality End	3:29:11PM	40°	233°
Eclipse End	4:37:00PM	29°	249°
Sunset	7:30:00PM	0°	281°

Lake Ontario

Elevation: 243 feet
Main road/hwy: US 167

Overview

Covering a significant portion of the border of Upstate New York with Canada, Lake Ontario is a unique location to watch the total eclipse from. This smallest of the Great Lakes is still a massive body of water with over seven hundred miles of shoreline. Note that the total eclipse will be in the southwestern sky, so you will be looking away from the water in many areas. The cities from Cape Vincent to Pulaski will have eclipse views mostly over the water. The centerline of the eclipse travels over Lake Ontario as it does Lake Erie. Be aware that both lakes have suffered flooding in spring from the snowmelt, so read local news sources and plan well ahead for the total eclipse.

Getting There

Travel to the major cities of Niagara Falls, Rochester, Oswego, and Watertown to begin your trek along Lake Ontario.

Totality Duration

Varies significantly depending on location.

Notes

Times are for Oswego. Times will vary significantly depending on your location on the lake.

Event	Time (EDT)	Altitude	Azimuth
Sunrise	6:34:00AM	0°	78°
Eclipse Start	2:08:44PM	51°	204°
Totality Start	3:21:37PM	43°	229°
Totality End	3:25:07PM	43°	230°
Eclipse End	4:34:22PM	32°	247°
Sunset	7:41:00PM	0°	281°

LAKE ERIE

Elevation: 569 feet
Main road/hwy: I-90

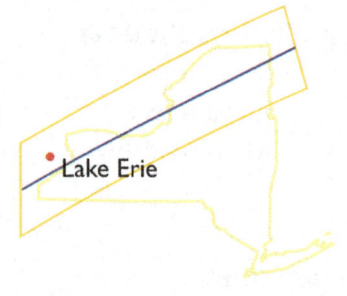

OVERVIEW
The fourth largest lake of the five Great Lakes of North America, it's also the smallest by volume of the lakes. That being said, Lake Erie packs a serious punch in terms of activities, sights, and fun for the whole family. Residents here enjoy the spectacular views, culture, and fun that the lake provides. Lake Erie is definitely the place to do it. Like Lake Ontario, the waterfront should be an excellent place to view the total eclipse, as the water will help cool the atmosphere, reducing distortion and providing a clearer view of the total eclipse. Note the eclipse will be in the southwest sky, so standing on most of the shore will have you looking away from the water.

GETTING THERE
Travel to the city of Buffalo then on to the lake or head southwest to the many cities along the shoreline.

TOTALITY DURATION
Varies depending on location.

NOTES
Times are for Westfield. Different locations will have different times.

Event	Time (EDT)	Altitude	Azimuth
Sunrise	6:48:00AM	0°	79°
Eclipse Start	2:03:16PM	54°	198°
Totality Start	3:17:03PM	46°	225°
Totality End	3:20:45PM	46°	226°
Eclipse End	4:31:17PM	35°	244°
Sunset	7:52:00PM	0°	281°

Remember the New York Total Eclipse
April 8, 2024

Who was I with? _____
_____
_____
_____
_____

What did I see? _____
_____
_____
_____
_____
_____
_____
_____
_____

What did I feel? _____
_____
_____
_____
_____
_____
_____
_____
_____

_____
_____
_____
_____

What did the people with me think? _____
_____
_____
_____
_____
_____
_____
_____
_____
_____

Where did I stay?_____
_____
_____
_____
_____
_____
_____
_____
_____

Enjoy Other Books by Aaron Linsdau

50 Jackson Hole Photography Hotspots
This guide reveals the best Jackson Hole photography spots. Learn what locals and insiders know to find the most impressive and iconic photography locations in the United States. This is an excellent companion guide to the *Jackson Hole Hiking Guide*.
www.sastrugipress.com/books/50-jackson-hole-photography-hotspots/

Adventure Expedition One
by Aaron Linsdau M.S. & Terry Williams, M.D.
Create, finance, enjoy, and return safely from your first expedition. Learn the techniques explorers use to achieve their goals and have a good time doing it. Acquire the skills, find the equipment, learn to camp, understand medical issues, and learn the planning necessary to pull off an expedition.
www.sastrugipress.com/books/adventure-expedition-one/

Antarctic Tears
Experience the honest story of solo polar exploration. This inspirational true book will make readers both cheer and cry. Coughing up blood and fighting skin-freezing temperatures were only a few of the perils Aaron Linsdau faced. Travel with him on a world-record expedition to the South Pole.
www.sastrugipress.com/books/antarctic-tears/

How to Keep Your Feet Warm in the Cold
Keep your feet warm in cold conditions on chilly adventures with techniques described in this book. Packed with dozens and dozens of ideas, learn how to avoid having cold feet ever again in your outdoor pursuits.
www.sastrugipress.com/books/how-to-keep-your-feet-warm-in-the-cold/

Jackson Hole Hiking Guide
Jackson Hole contains some of the most dramatic and iconic landscapes in the United States. The book shares everything you need to know to hike Jackson's classic trails with canyons, high mountains, and hidden alpine lakes. This book is an excellent companion guide to *50 Jackson Hole Photography Hotspots*.
www.sastrugipress.com/books/jackson-hole-hiking-guide/

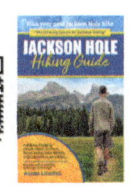

Subscribe to Aaron's YouTube channel at www.youtube.com/@alinsdau

If you enjoyed this book, please consider leaving a five-star review and a few words on what you liked about it at your favorite online retailer.

Lost at Windy Corner

Windy Corner on Denali has claimed fingers, toes, and even lives. What would make someone brave lethal weather, crevasses, and avalanches to attempt to summit North America's highest mountain? Aaron Linsdau shares the experience of climbing Denali alone and how you can apply the lessons to your life.
www.sastrugipress.com/books/lost-windy-corner/

The Motivated Amateur's Guide to Winter Camping

Winter camping is one of the most satisfying ways to experience the wilderness. It is also the most challenging style of overnighting in the outdoors. Learn 100+ tips from a professional polar explorer on how to winter camp safely and be comfortable in the cold.
www.sastrugipress.com/books/the-motivated-amateurs-guide-to-winter-camping/

Two Friends and a Polar Bear
by Terry Williams, M.D. & Aaron Linsdau

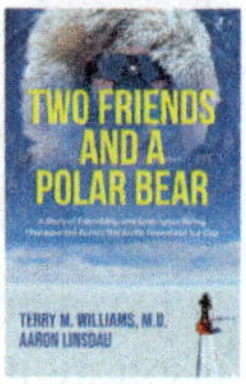

This story of friendship is about two old friends who plan to ski across the Greenland Ice Cap along the Arctic Circle in hopes of becoming one of the oldest teams to succeed.
www.sastrugipress.com/books/two-friends-and-a-polar-bear/

About the Author

Aaron Linsdau is the second American to ski alone from the coast of Antarctica to the South Pole (730 miles / 1174 km), setting a world record for surviving the longest expedition ever for that trip. He lead a 310-mile (499 km) ski expedition across the Greenland icecap along the Arctic Circle. Aaron has climbed Denali solo, crossed the Greenland tundra alone, skied across Yellowstone National Park solo, trekked through the Sahara desert, and successfully climbed Mt. Kilimanjaro and Mt. Elbrus in Russia.

Aaron Linsdau at the South Pole.

Use your smart device to scan the QR codes for website links.

Visit www.aaronlinsdau.com/subscribe to learn more about the author. Receive updates when he releases new books and shows.

Visit Sastrugi Press on the web at www.sastrugipress.com to purchase the above titles in bulk. They are available in print, e-book, or audiobook form.

Thank you for choosing Sastrugi Press.

Enjoy Other Books by Sastrugi Press

50 Florida Wildlife Hotspots by Moose Henderson Ph.D.

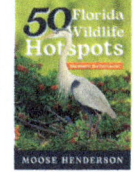

This is a definitive guide to finding where to photograph wildlife in Florida. Follow the guidance of a professional wildlife photographer as he takes you to some of the best places to see wildlife in the Sunshine State.
www.sastrugipress.com/books/50-florida-wildlife-hotspots/

50 Wildlife Hotspots Grand Teton National Park by Moose Henderson Ph.D.

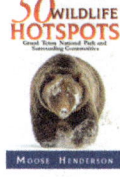

Find out where to find animals and photograph them in Grand Teton National Park from a professional wildlife photographer. Learn techniques, timing, animal behavior, and composition to create stunning wildlife images.
www.sastrugipress.com/books/50-wildlife-hotspots/

Alaska: A Guide for the Curious by Nikki Mann & Jeff Wohl

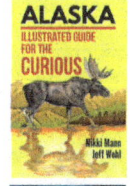

Discover the natural world of Alaska. Find out what the plants and animals are like, how to identify them, and what the environment of Alaska is like.
www.sastrugipress.com/books/alaska-a-guide-for-the-curious/

Blood Justice by Tim W. James

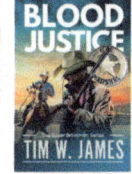

Two brothers, one a preacher's son, the other an adopted would-be slave, set out in opposite directions to avenge their family's murder only to cross paths in pursuit of the killer. Book 1 of the Roger Brinkman Series.
www.sastrugipress.com/iron-spike-press/blood-justice/

Shake Yourself Free by Bob Millsap

Learn how to overcome difficult encounters with misfortune, tragedy, and loss. Emotional recovery is a journey requiring a mindset shift. Get this book now and take control of your life.
www.sastrugipress.com/books/shake-yourself-free/

The Burqa Cave by Dean Petersen

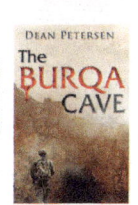

Still haunted by Iraq, a retired soldier seeks solace teaching high school in Wyoming. He soon finds the quiet town is home to murderers, maniacs, and a boy who can see where missing murder victims are. This paranormal thriller-romance surprises readers with unexpected twists.
www.sastrugipress.com/books/the-burqa-cave/

Photography Notes

April 8, 2024

Settings _____
_____
_____
_____
_____

Successes _____
_____
_____
_____
_____
_____
_____

Challenges _____
_____
_____
_____
_____
_____
_____

Photography Notes
April 8, 2024

Camera _____
_____
_____
_____
_____
_____

Company _____
_____
_____
_____
_____
_____
_____
_____
_____

Location _____
_____
_____
_____
_____
_____
_____
_____
_____

Made in the USA
Coppell, TX
03 April 2024